W9-CHF-294

INSTITUTIONAL BARRIERS TO POLAND'S ECONOMIC DEVELOPMENT

Poland's transition from socialism to capitalism has largely been praised as a success story. In reality, however, according to this study, Poland's case is an 'incomplete' transition. There are many indicators of this: the resistance to the institution-building of a capitalist market economy; there is no constitution reaffirming private property rights as a cornerstone of an economic system; privatization is lagging behind most post-communist countries and reprivatization has not even been touched; factor markets are either underdeveloped, and becoming distorted in the process, or have been severely distorted from the start; and welfarism is rampant, second only to Hungary, and unsustainable in the medium to long term.

The authors argue that these symptoms arise from a political economy failure to build the required institutions, once the initial enthusiasm waned, and the positive effects of those initial measures – which began the process in the early 1990s – petered out. These essays suggest respective economic remedies, and demonstrate why some of them are politically difficult in the present, still volatile, political climate. Moreover, they tentatively look at the sources of resistance to further systematic change which go beyond traditional 'reform fatigue'.

The book looks at the processes involved in economic transition, covering key issues including financial markets, labour market, competition and intervention, social security, property rights and attitudes towards the changing political economy. It provides a wide-ranging and invaluable study of economic development, and will be of great use to economists, those involved in Russian and East European studies and to political scientists.

Jan Winiecki is Professor of Economics at the European University–Viadrina, Germany, and Vice-President of the Polish Society of Market Economists. A former member of Walesa's political advisory committee, he was the founder and first president of the free market think-tank Adam Smith Research Center, and Executive Director of the European Bank for Reconstruction and Development. He has three books published by Routledge, most recently as the co-editor, with A. Kondratowicz, of *The Macroeconomics of Transition: Developments in East-Central Europe* (1993).

ROUTLEDGE STUDIES OF SOCIETIES IN TRANSITION

INSTITUTIONAL BARRIERS TO POLAND'S ECONOMIC DEVELOPMENT

The incomplete transition

Edited by Jan Winiecki

London and New York

First published 1997
by Routledge
11 New Fetter Lane, London EC4P 4EE

Simultaneously published in the USA and Canada
by Routledge
29 West 35th Street, New York, NY 10001

Typeset in Garamond by RefineCatch Limited, Bungay, Suffolk

Printed and bound in Great Britain by
Redwood Books, Trowbridge, Wiltshire

British Library Cataloguing in Publication Data
A catalogue record for this book is available from the British Library

Library of Congress Cataloging in Publication Data
Institutional barriers to economic development: Poland's incomplete
transition / edited by Jan Winiecki.
p.   cm.
'First published 1996 as Monograph no. 26 by Adam Smith Research
Centre, Warsaw, as the final report for the International Center for Economic
Growth, San Francisco'—T.p. verso.
Includes bibliographical references (p. 104) and index.
(hardbound)
1. Privatization—Poland.   2. Poland—Economic policy—1990–   .
3. Poland—Economic conditions—1990–   .   I. Winiecki, Jan.
HC340.3.I568   1997
338.9438—dc21   97–6091

ISBN 0–415–16301–3

CONTENTS

CONTENTS

CONTRIBUTORS

Antoni Z. Kamiński is a professor at the Institute of Political Science, Warsaw University. He is also a member of the Board of Directors of the Adam Smith Research Center, Warsaw.

Jan Stefanowicz is a lawyer and the chairman of *Juris*, a law firm specializing in business law-related issues.

Jacek Szymanderski is a political sociologist and public opinion expert, consultant at the Central Statistical Office. He is also a former MP and President of the OBOP (a Polish polling organization).

Aleksandra Wiktorow is a senior researcher on social policy and social security issues at the Institute for the Study of Market Economy, Gdańsk (Danzig). She is the former Deputy Minister for Labor and Social Affairs.

Jan Winiecki is the professor and chair of International Trade and Finance at the European University–Viadrina, Frankfurt an der Oder. He is founder and the first president of the Adam Smith Research Center, and a former member of President Wałęsa's Political Advisory Committee.

PREFACE

This book has been made possible due to the interest of the Center for International Economic Growth (ICEG) in East-Central Europe's transition from socialist, centrally-administered to capitalist, market-driven economy. Within the area Poland was singled out as a rather curious case of a 'not quite' or 'incomplete' success story. As perceived from the other side of the Atlantic, obstacles to making Poland a complete success story were (rightly!) thought to be first of all institutional.

Stabilization measures succeeded in throttling near-hyperinflation inherited from communist times and later reduced (ever more slowly) the rate of inflation. Liberalization measures resulted in the reestablishing of the rudiments of the market economy almost overnight. Within the framework of the liberalization, the furthest-reaching deregulation stimulated the expansion of the generic private sector – and with it the surge in economic growth (after an unavoidable transformational recession). However, the institution-building going beyond rudiments of the market encountered resistance. The new Constitution establishing the foundations of the capitalist market system, with private property as a dominant form of ownership, has not materialized. Privatization encountered fierce resistance from most quarters. Reprivatization has not been even agreed upon by the major political forces, with Poland being the only country in the region that did not implement one or another reprivatization scheme. Competition, external and increasingly also internal, has been ever more limited by the increasingly activist state.

To identify the major obstacles and recommend ways of coping with them, the project: 'Institutional Barriers to Poland's Economic Development' has been elaborated in the Adam Smith Research

Center in Warsaw, under the aegis of the then-President of the Center, Professor Jan Winiecki. Approved of and generously financed by ICEG, it resulted in a large number of working papers covering various aspects of the Polish institutional framework and economic policies. A group of analysts working on the Final Report from the project have benefited from that accumulated knowledge (in fact, working papers themselves aroused a lot of interest, reflected in their coverage in Polish daily and professional economics and business journals).

The Final Report generated interest not only in Poland but also abroad, with Routledge, the publisher of the report being a conspicuous example. Thus, our thanks go to both the International Center for Economic Growth and Routledge who together made the report and the book possible. And, on a more personal note, we would like to extend our thanks to the late George A. Truitt, ICEG's East European Adviser, whose friendly but incisive comments, offered in his typical quiet way, were extremely helpful at various stages of the project.

The Authors

ACKNOWLEDGEMENT
A note on the text

This book was first published in 1996 as Monograph No. 26 of the Adam Smith Research Center, Warsaw, as the *Final Report for the International Center for Economic Growth*, San Francisco. Professor Jan Winiecki was the project coordinator.

The project, sponsored by the International Center for Economic Growth, has been financed with the funds received by the ICEG from The Pew Charitable Trusts.

The opinions expressed in the project's report are those of the authors and do not necessarily reflect the views of The Pew Charitable Trusts.

1

INTRODUCTION
Seven years' experience
Jan Winiecki

In 1989 it became obvious even for the politically blind that the combination of communist political monopoly and socialist economic institutions had finally run its course. Poland was the first country of Eastern Europe where a visible break with the past had taken place. Political change preceded economic change. It could not have been otherwise. With the important segments of the ruling stratum that lived off the economic subsystem situated at the center of political power, only political change could abolish *nomenklatura* and establish a real (rather than phony) market system. Thus, the establishment of the first non-communist government opened the window of opportunity: the probability (but not the certainty!) of the successful change to a capitalist, private ownership-based market economy.

The initial reform package conceived in late 1989 gave the economy a strong push in the right direction. The package consisted of a set of stabilizing, liberalizing and market institution-building measures (including privatization) that on the whole did not differ from the standard sets usually recommended by international financial institutions. Thus, the new government:

1 introduced a set of stabilizing macroeconomic measures, setting a restrictive course for the monetary policy and reducing sharply budgetary subsidies for both producers and (somewhat less sharply) for consumers;
2 liberalized domestic wholesale and consumer prices (up to 85–90 percent of the total);
3 freed domestic and international trade from controls;
4 established a unified exchange rate (pegged first to the dollar and later to a basket of currencies);

5 passed a set of changes in the existing laws that regulate economic activity, reaffirming the freedom of entrepreneurship and the freedom of contracting;

6 extended the independence of state enterprises (except for the wage setting process that has been regulated by wage controls); and

7 announced the beginning of the process of privatization.

The fact that the package is largely standardized has had twofold consequences. On the one hand it ensured a certain degree of consistency between various measures. On the other, by neglecting first of all the heritage of the socialist past, it did not take into account certain features of the old economic system that might have affected (and did affect) the course of transition (on this point see Winiecki 1993b and 1995a). Nonetheless there have been some measures within the set that went further and it is these measures that put Poland in the forefront of East European countries in transition. Thus, Poland went the furthest in ensuring the freedom of entry for the private sector to almost any area of economic activity. Also, it went further than envisaged by the standard International Monetary Fund–World Bank package in opening up the economy to international trade (thanks to the influence of Jeffrey Sachs).

The former gave Polish economy an unusual dynamism that resulted in a faster expansion of the private sector than elsewhere in the post-communist world in spite of the sluggish privatization process. Even leaving aside agriculture (which remained largely private even during communist years) the share of the private sector in GDP already exceeded 50 percent by 1993. The latter substituted for the initially weak domestic competition by putting strong pressure on domestic producers to adjust to the demands of the fast-changing domestic market.

However, it should have been obvious for politicians and analysts alike that the measures introduced on 1 January 1990 or started in the early months of that year are but an initial, minimally consistent set of measures, designed and introduced to 'get the ball rolling' (Winiecki 1989). The emergence of a new economic order (any order, in fact) is a slow process that evolves according to its own – largely unpredictable – dynamics. The state cannot plan or control it according to minute details of some blueprint. This is the point hammered home again and again by a theorist-turned-practitioner,

Vaclav Klaus, the prime minister of the Czech Republic (and by other reformers, such as New Zealander Roger Douglas, an architect of the most free market-oriented reform in the West). The best that the state can hope for is to create the most conducive environment for the process to evolve (Hockuba 1995). Such a conducive environment for the capitalist market system is, then, dependent primarily on: first, the process of building the necessary market institutions, including the set of market- and private property-enhancing laws; second, the efficiency of the law enforcement, particularly important for the capitalist market economy on the one hand and particularly difficult to achieve in the unstable, chaotic conditions of transition; and finally, privatization (including reprivatization) of the state sector aimed at reducing the role of the inefficient owner in the economy and reducing the extent of the political rather than market-based allocation of resources (as the latter is less conflict-prone and disturbing to the process of economic growth). The satisfactorily efficient capitalist market economy emerges only at a certain stage of that process, when the gap between the supply of and demand for the institutions narrows substantially. Another condition is the adjustment of economic agents who learn the new market rules of behavior, so to say, on the job. Clearly, however, the speed of their adjustment to rules is dependent *ceteris paribus* on the existence of rules themselves.

But it is here that Polish transition had already begun to splutter some years ago. On the institution-building side, the initial strong push has not been followed with the necessary degree of consistency later on. To begin with, Poland after eight years of deliberation got a new constitution, where the fundamentals of the capitalist market order were not well established. Worse still, as it will be shown later in the report, what has been passed is too amorphous to be in concordance with *any* economic order, not necessarily a private ownership-based market economy. And Article 1 states, uniquely in post-communist East-Central Europe, that the Polish Republic implements the 'principles of social justice', a typical communist slogan of extremely vague content, and therefore, again, open to any interpretation of a transient parliamentary majority.

The foregoing might not have been such a drawback if the necessary set of laws and organizations had been established in the ordinary law-making process. It did not happen, however. To give a striking example, even the fundamental principle of the capitalist market order, that of private property, has not been legally upheld until now. The most visible is the case of reprivatization. Poland has been the only East-Central European country not to have passed a reprivatization law. Not only has unlawfully-taken private property not been returned to its lawful owners, but even the privatization of state-established enterprises has encountered fiercer resistance from both political left and right in Poland than anywhere else in the East-Central European region. Even the privatization ministry (everywhere so called) has, in Poland, been named the Ministry for Ownership Transformation (Ministerstwo Przekształceń Własnościowych) by the first non-communist government of Mr Mazowiecki to appease political forces suspicious of and/or hostile to privatization.

A special note has to be devoted to the distortions of both the spirit and the letter of capitalist institution-building under the reign of the ex-communist coalition. Apart from the (expected) tilt toward more intervention, the ex-communist coalition that came to power in 1993 creates laws in a manner not markedly different from that characteristic of the old communist regime. Namely, they draft laws in such a way as to leave unlimited discretion in the hands of the executive apparatus. Thus, the protection of citizens' rights, normally offered by acts of parliament (that is by the legislature), is next to non-existent as laws passed by parliament are but empty shells, while all the burdens borne by citizens as taxpayers, entrepreneurs, etc., are decided – in a more or less uncontrolled manner – at the level of the executive.

Cases of the already-passed law on public procurement, with its 45 delegations of important powers to different parts of the executive, or the draft of the tax code presented to the parliament, with its 38 delegations to the Minister of Finance alone, are just the most conspicuous among the whole avalanche of recent and current legislative initiatives of the ex-communist coalition.

The unlimited discretion has twofold aims. First, discretion creates room for political favoritism. Taxes postponed or foregone, preferential credits or guaranteed credits, public contracts given without due tendering process – all this, and a lot more, may keep inefficient state firms going and bring political rewards. And the public enterprise sector, together with the so-called 'budget sector' (education, health, public administration), and agriculture as another budget-dependent sector, are the political stronghold of the ex-communist coalition. Second, by leaving public officials, rather than transparent rules, in control of the decision process, discretion

creates the room for private enrichment. And if the rules are struc-
tured in such a way that public officials make decisions not only with
respect to the class of cases but with respect to individual cases,
the room for corruption becomes even bigger. The activities of
that sort are so profitable – both politically and personally – that
the number of concessions, quotas, etc. has been multiplying
like locusts in the desert. In the foreign trade area alone there are
now permissions, exclusions, quotas, concessions, etc., affecting
about 4,000 product groups (approximately 25 percent of Polish
imports).

A spate of currently prepared legislative initiatives goes even
further and looks like a planned effort to create room for both.
Quite a few institutions envisaged in these initiatives will offer wide
opportunities in these respects. A number of agencies – created or
to be created – at the borderline of the state and the market are
ideally suited for such a role. They are financed from the state
budget, but operate – often on a large scale – in the market. Thus,
they offer the dual opportunity to spend resources in an
uncontrolled manner on political clientele, while at the same time
influence market developments (to the benefit of those in control
of the decision process – and privileged information). Other institutions are so designed as to offer a number of well-paid jobs to the
members of the old communist ruling stratum that has not yet
found its way back to the apparatus of the state. The need of a
market economy for both types of institutions, let alone their
design, may be questioned.

The foregoing distorted institutional development has two
strongly adverse consequences. Thus, it is the expanding private
sector outside agriculture – the mainstay of Polish transition – that
will pay the triple price of: first, costs of increasing intervention in
the private sector; second, indirectly, the cost of increasing transfer
of resources to the economically inefficient but politically important
state enterprise sector; and third, costs of corruption plain and
simple. Furthermore, a variety of state agencies are licensed to
operate on the market creating the room for hidden renationalization through the role of the Treasury agents on the stock market, as
well as through other state agencies potentially extending controls
over private economic agents. This scope for hidden renationalization through market methods has been created at the same time as
privatization has been continuing at a very slow pace (even slower
than during successive non-communist governments). This has

been to some extent the consequence of the policy makers' mistaken preferences for privatization through the classical, well-proven methods of public sale and direct sale to interested parties. As these methods have been organizationally-intensive (in the sense of Levy 1993), the ability of the state apparatus to go fast through the complicated process requiring a network of the many participating private agents and public institutions, turned out to be predictably slow. Privatization 'shortcuts' have been resisted and, when introduced on a small scale (Polish mass privatization program – PPP), pursued rather halfheartedly and amidst many political quarrels. The only alternative to the classical privatization envisaged by the law, that is leasing of enterprise assets, became the favored vehicle of the trade unions and employees in establishing the least efficient form of private ownership, that is closed employee-owned companies.

With privatization proceeding at a slow pace, the stock market has remained a little more than a marginal institution with no more than a few dozen quoted companies. Of course, one might have expected purely private firms to enter the stock market but here a more general problem of the underdevelopment of the financial markets has played its role. As freedom of entry for private firms has not been matched by improved access to capital markets, private firms often face strong barriers to the expansion that would allow them to achieve a scale of economic activity to make them suitable candidates for entering the stock market.

Just as the privatization of industrial enterprises proceeded slowly, so that of banks has barely started. The state-owned banks continue to dominate the scene and (as shown in the section on financial markets) even those formally privatized are dominated by the government through Treasury-held major shareholdings. Moreover, investment banking is only beginning to find its place in the Polish financial sector. This has an additional adverse effect on the restructuring ability of the enterprise sector. In the ruling ex-communist coalition and in the large segments of political opposition, there has been a considerable reluctance to allow foreign banks to enter both commercial and investment banking. The reluctance of the authorities is, unfortunately, matched by an even stronger anti-foreign investment bias among large parts of the general public – a bias that extends to *all* (not only banking) foreign investment.

It seems necessary at this point to signal the interaction between the political economy of Polish transition and the institution-building as this has been the prime source of the incompleteness of the institutional side of the process in question. The uniqueness of Polish transition in comparison with other Central and East European countries lies in the fact that the political change has been accomplished by the 'Solidarity' political movement which has been largely utopian socialist cum syndicalist in its nature. The prime consequence has been that the Polish political spectrum is strongly anti-capitalist at both ends, with an ex-communist alliance (Sojusz Lewicy Demokratycznej – SLD) and its anachronistic peasant ally (Polskie Stronnictwo Ludowe – PSL) at one end and the strongly anti-communist but utopian Christian-socialist 'Solidarity' at the other. To give an example: a public opinion survey of the liberal, free market-oriented strategy brought about 70 percent of negative opinions within the ranks of SLD sympathizers, 73 percent within the PSL and 80 percent within the 'Solidarity' electorate (*Życie Gospodarcze* 1994, No. 34)! The modern core of the body politic dominant in the West – from social democrats on the left to Christian democrats and conservatives on the right – is relatively weak.

In consequence, once the period of 'extraordinary politics' (see Balcerowicz 1993), with its strong public support for change, ended and the 'reform fatigue' (see Bruno 1992) set in, the process of institution-building, including privatization, has been stalled. Reprivatization and privatization have been early victims but soon, so were other necessary measures shaping the factor markets. Political difficulties coupled with unwillingness to accept extensive foreign presence constrained the rapid expansion of the financial markets. The unequal strength of labor and capital has also been one of the root causes of the distorted institutional arrangements on the labor market. The imbalance between the power of labor and capital, to the distinct disadvantage of the latter, is a fixed point of the political economy of Polish transition. The imbalance stems from the fact that both political camps, ex-communists and 'Solidarity' trade union, draw their numerical strength from the same sectors of the economy, that is the state enterprise sector and the so-called 'budget sector' (health, education, public administration). Both are much better organized than employers' organizations in the private sector outside agriculture and, therefore, organized labor is politically superior regardless of who is in power.

There are important and highly disadvantageous economic consequences of this imbalance (not only political but also legal, as exemplified in the Polish labor code by the right to strike but no right to lock-out), quite apart from its role as a deterrent to foreign investment. Polish wages are extremely sticky downwards and the willingness to trade wage cuts for higher employment is almost non-existent (in contrast to the Czech Republic). State-owned loss-making enterprises dominate in some branches of industry, forcing wage increases regardless of the economic situation. All this inter-acts with relatively lenient eligibility criteria for unemployment benefits. The result is high unemployment, underpinned by the very rigid labor market, with low occupational and territorial mobility, as well as a high reservation wage for the unemployed, approaching 95 percent of the last wage (even after two years of unemployment, see Góra 1994). Therefore, the high economic growth rate of the 1993–95 period – expected to last for another year or two – did not make much of a dent in the unemployment rate under the circumstances in question (aggravated by the very high taxation of the factor labor).

The issues of the fundamental reform of what is called the 'budget sector' (in the West called properly the public sector) and of the social security system – political minefields even in more stable democracies – have so far always been left for the future in Polish transition. The political economy of Polish transition mentioned earlier creates a pathological situation with trade union demands for salary increases first, and reforms later. However, as reform pro-posals are predicated on an improved efficiency in these badly per-formed and highly overstaffed services, pay increases reduce whatever willingness is there in these sectors to reform themselves. So far no government, regardless of the size of its parliamentary majority, has been ready to tackle these problems – and trade unions – head-on.

Somewhat more active have been some transition-period governments in the case of the social security system. Reform attempts and proposals in this respect have been due, not so much to the greater foresight of politicians, but to the more pressing nature of the problem. They, thus, confirm the favored dictum of the American businessman and politician George Schultz, who is fond of saying that 'if things get bad enough, people will do even the most obvious and sensible things'. Thus, it is obvious that the social security system in Poland cannot continue for long in its present form. Poland, at best a middle-developed economy, spends on pensions more than any other European country, East or West. The share of pensions in Polish GDP has been about 15 percent in the mid-1990s. The next highest share in GDP of an East-Central

European country, is in Hungary, 11–11.5 percent (still substantially more than the average share for European Union countries: 8.7 percent in 1992). And the growth of the pensions' share in the transition period has been financed almost exclusively through an increase in budgetary subsidies.

Pensions are in Poland on the average much higher than in other countries: 70 percent of average wage and salary rather than the 40–50 percent of most European countries, East and West. Moreover, pensioners not only get higher pensions but get them for much longer as they are younger than elsewhere due to earlier retirement, except perhaps in Italy (another country with an extremely costly and wasteful social security system, also urgently requiring institutional changes). Furthermore, the system is saddled with the duty to deliver hidden social assistance to farmers under the guise of a pension system (for it is definitely not a pension system, where farmers' contributions amount to barely 5 percent of total expenditures).

Some attempts to stem the flood of expenditures were made as early as 1991. The effects of these measures will, however, be slow in coming. Thus, a more fundamental reform is necessary. Since there are no political kamikaze ready to propose the radical downward adjustment of pensions to the levels found elsewhere), reform outlines concentrate on setting the principles of the system based on three separate but intertwined pillars:

1 uniform basic pension for everybody;
2 contribution-based pension (with the introduction of pension funds or, in more timid proposals, without); and
3 individual pension plans.

Any reform will require an increased budgetary funding throughout the rather long transition period from one system to another. The second pillar is the core of success. The contributions-based component of pensions seems easier to finance because pension funds will then use contributions to obtain at least minimal returns (see Mech 1995 and Topiński 1996). Other analysts are more cautious and their cautiousness is reinforced by the well-known political economy of the pension reform. The process of reform has been, moreover, made even more complicated due to the fact that some sectoral measures already undertaken by the present ex-communist coalition make the transition even more difficult and costly in the future, as shown in Chapter 6 (see also Gomułka 1996).

Probably the most adverse consequences of the political change since 1993 have been felt in the area of competition and the openness toward the external world. What we registered here has been a marked change in the philosophy of economic governance in this respect. It has been conveniently forgotten, or not understood in the first place, that the position of Poland as an economic growth leader in the post-communist world has been mainly due to the fact that the first Polish non-communist governments went further in both domestic deregulation and opening the Polish economy to world market stimuli. This created room for expansion of the generic private sector that, consequently, grew at unprecedented rates, so that it now produces more than half of GDP. The strength of the Polish private sector outside agriculture – in reality *the only* dynamic sector of Polish economy – has been built on twin principles of competition and openness. And it is this strength that is being eroded by the past and current infringements on these basic principles of the capitalist market economy.

It is true that the first protectionist measures had already been undertaken in late 1991 and have been growing ever since. But the return of political forces steeped in the philosophy of command and interference from the center in the operation of the economy heralds *qualitative* change. Under non-communist governments protectionist or domestic competition limiting measures were undertaken under pressure from interest groups. Now, intervention seems to be the principle rather than an exception. Thus, the openness of the economy has been significantly eroded, with one area after another being more or less shielded from foreign competition. There has been a general rise in the level of tariff protection since 1991. Agriculture comes first, with high non-tariff and tariff barriers, but a whole range of products from cars and consumer electronics to food products is being affected by various import impediments. As noted already in a different context, about one fourth of Polish imports is now subject to various non-tariff barriers: quotas, exceptions from quotas, concessions, etc. Non-tariff barriers did not omit exports, either (although on a smaller scale).

At the same time 'industrial policy' sprang back into fashion in its most crude and obsolete forms. In Chapter 5 we stress the singular inappropriateness of industrial policies as pursued in the West and/ or the developing countries. What we note here, however, is the fact that the ex-communist coalition added another twist to the limitations of competition and openness, namely a centralization of the economy and, therefore, the limitation also of internal competition. All these coal trusts, sugar trusts, coupled with the already implemented or discussed ideas of the 'consolidation' of state banks, establishment or encouragement of various holdings, have twofold aims. On the one hand they are to shield the inefficient state enterprise sector from efficiency demands of the market and thereby earning the gratitude of its political clientele employed there. On the other, they are to retain the state sector as an important spoils area for the old *nomenklatura* from both parties of the communist *ancien régime*.

Such policies, apart from making the private enterprise sector less responsive to the demands of the market both directly (through increased cost of distorted competition) and indirectly (through more limited access to factors and markets) are also harmful for the protected state sector. As the treaty with the European Union also obliges the Polish side to annually reduce tariff levels and eliminate non-tariff barriers, the rise in the level of protection and the general unpreparedness of the state sector for international competition may, in the not-too-distant future, threaten that sector with near-extinction. Thus, either that area of political favoritism and personal aggrandizement will disappear, or the ruling coalition, following its sectional interests, will postpone our entry into the European Union. Given the ex-communists' record, it seems obvious that they are sacrificing the interests of the nation and the national economy rather than their own.

To sum up, budding economic activity of the generic private sector, registered and unregistered alike, has put Poland in the forefront of transition. However, without sufficient, well-proven institutional underpinnings, the increasingly efficiently working markets will never materialize and temporary successes will run out of steam. The following chapters survey the areas where institutional barriers are most glaringly visible and may particularly strongly – and adversely – affect future performance.

2

BUILDING INSTITUTIONS IN THE THIRD REPUBLIC

A distorted rule-making process

Antoni Z. Kamiński and Jan Stefanowicz

The advancement and implementation of institutional changes associated with the transition from communism to a liberal democracy are occurring on two interrelated planes: the transition from a single-party monopoly to multi-party pluralism, with all the implications for establishing a political system, and the transition from a centrally administered economy to a market economy. From the point of view of the society, this is a revolution, for it is changing the basis of the hitherto existing order for what is the reverse of the political and economic past.

Errors in establishing the political institutions not only cause the instability of a political system but also affect the setting of priorities and quality of legislation. We would note, however, that although the economy may adjust to political distortions and – at least for the time being – effectively nullify their impact, in the long term an adjustment to distortions results in a distorted economy.

The nature of the relationship between politics and economics during a transitional period stems from the fact that the process of transition is, quite naturally, political in character, i.e. new economic institutions are established on the basis of political decisions. The basic problem for each elite trying to bring about changes in the political system, or assuming responsibility for designing and implementing any comprehensive political program, is to correctly determine priorities. The period during which society shows a considerable plasticity, i.e. when it is ready to accept far-reaching changes, is usually short. During such a period, new interest groups have not yet been formed, old ones are often in disarray, and thus the reform activities on the one hand enjoy general support, while on the other specific arrangements do not, as yet, encounter strong resistance. Afterwards, the society will continue to support the reforms in general terms. However, in particular cases, threatening group interests, changes will be (often fiercely) resisted.

Without questioning what was called by Popper a 'piecemeal change method' and by Lindblom 'muddling through' decisions, it seems necessary to properly formulate the constitutional framework within which spontaneous activities occur. This framework may be created in hundreds of years, sometimes with positive effects, as in the case of British democracy. However, in the case of modern systemic changes, their successes largely depended on the existence of a preceding general concept of a new order. Examples abound: the successful Prussian reforms carried out in the eighteenth and nineteenth centuries, the Constitution of the United States, the Meiji restoration in Japan, or the reforms of the Great Sejm in Poland in the eighteenth century (although in the last example they failed to succeed because of a foreign invasion).

The 'constitutional moment' has, unfortunately, passed in Poland, without much being done in this respect. One of the reasons was that the new political elite, despite undoubtedly democratic convictions, preferred a 'movement in support of reform', rather than serious thinking about the creation of a new political and economic order. To paraphrase a well-known saying, the movement was everything whereas the concept was nothing (Kamiński and Kurczewska 1994). Hence, the process of making the Constitution was inappropriately approached from the very beginning. Instead of establishing one body, the purpose of which would be to prepare a concise text, two independent working groups were established: the Constitutional Committees of the Sejm and Senate. What is more, different political parties, citizens' groups, and the Office of the President of the Republic of Poland, began preparing their own projects. The factor that influenced the pace of work on the Constitution was a rather common belief that the Sejm elected in July 1989, as a result of a deal between the communist authorities and opposition should not be the one to pass the new Constitution. Thus, everyone waited for more than two years for a new Sejm to be elected. However, once that happened in 1991, it made no progress regarding the Constitution.

The issue was additionally complicated by the infighting within the victorious anti-communist opposition. The issue of who was going to manage the process of systemic change became, for many, more important than their subject matter. Their minds were dominated not by the problem of what to do with the power they had but who was going to be in the position of power. Such was the essence of the so-called 'war at the top' for which all groupings involved share responsibility. Rather than dissolve the Sejm in the Spring of 1990 and hold parliamentary elections as soon as possible to consolidate political gains of 1989 and, then, begin a coherent constitutional process, presidential elections by means of a nation-wide vote were held first. Ironically, those who derailed the political process in this manner did not gain politically; on the contrary, they lost – and with them the whole victorious democratic movement.

Consequently, until Spring 1997, when the Constitution was finally passed and approved in a referendum, the so-called 'Small Constitution', a modified version of the communist Constitution, dealt with the systemic fundamentals of the Third Republic. However, the *ad hoc* institutional arrangements introduced in 1991 did not solve basic systemic issues. We should bear in mind that the quality of a constitution influences the capability of the political system to realize the public interest. Not only the fact but also the way elections are held are important in democracy. One issue is worth noting in this respect. The electoral law based on proportional representation is conducive to the diffusion of political forces; therefore, to weaken its effects, thresholds are sometimes introduced (for example, parties which do not gain 5 percent of the vote do not enter the parliament).

It would seem that in the countries emerging from communism, an electoral law that forces the newly established political parties to cooperate at the pre-electoral stage should be introduced. This has not happened in Poland. The result was successive governments formed by loose coalitions of groups emerging from the former 'Solidarity' movement. However, given the corrosion of civilized political (and not only political!) behavior under communism, inter-party coordination within coalitions has strongly hindered the conduct of a coherent policy in any area. In numerical terms the presently ruling ex-communist coalition is seemingly in a better situation, although they operate under pressure of the same inheritance. This leads to a phenomenon called the 'feudalization of power', which implies the subordination of public functions within a system to the criteria of personal or sectional interests.

The tendencies described above lead also to the weakness of the state. The most apparent symptom of that weakness is the state's incapability to effectively resist the pressures of specific interests.

This is particularly noticeable in the case of trade unions and employees of large enterprises, the peasant parties, and the Catholic Church.

The political priorities of the Church have many times managed to draw the attention of the state away from the most urgent systemic issues. Rather than concentrate on systemic changes, parliamentarians were engaged in disputes over abortion and divorces, that is, over the issues important from a moral point of view, but not the most significant for a state which, within the last two hundred years, has twice disappeared from the maps of Europe, and over the last half-a-century existed as a vassal of a neighboring imperial power. Thus, once such a state has been given several years' breathing space, its political elites should primarily think how to strengthen its structures. Moral and religious revival constitute elements necessary for a revival of the nation, but they cannot be legislated by the state.

Another harmful development on the Polish political scene is the ability of employees in large state-owned enterprises and their union representatives to 'bring the state to its knees' (or at least to act as if they could). Therefrom stem concessions for employees with respect to privatization decisions, the absence of restraints on workplace labor protest, persistence of subsidies to loss-makers unwilling or unable to adapt, and so on. A vaguely defined role for labor unions aggravates the problems in question. They partly assumed the functions of political parties seeking grassroots support from employees, and therefore ready to back them in every labor conflict in order to gain their support.

The third case of particular interests which in the most recent period has made considerable gains at the expense of society as a whole, is the peasant party (PSL). It consists of the most opportunist elements on the Polish political stage. Their primary purpose as a party-in-power is to ensure the largest possible number of plum jobs in the state apparatus for party activists, and to extort, under the guise of agricultural and other policies, the most favorable arrangements for the communist-time apparatchiks controlling that party and for their electorate. The inability of the state to protect the common interest against the pressure of particular interests clearly indicates the weakness of its institutions.

The adverse effects of the foregoing would be somewhat less onerous if the reforms of public administration were not so neglected. Competent administration enables the state to function reasonably well even in the midst of political crisis. However, in all three very important areas little if anything has been done. First, a strict separation of political functions from administrative ones is a necessary condition for the administration to be efficient and competent. Nothing has happened in this respect and the return to power of the forces of the communist past made things much worse in this respect. Second, the recruitment of 'new blood' is very important and the recruited must come from among the best students in top universities. For this to happen, however, incentives must exist to attract them to public service. And, third, there must be established mechanisms of political and judicial control (internal oversight is not enough). Transparent and coherent legislation, as well as independence, competence, and efficiency of judiciary are important preconditions of such control.

Another thrust of administration reform should be its decentralization based on territorial self-government. At first, under the Mazowiecki government, two contrary tendencies surfaced. On the one hand, local governments were established, but on the other they were limited in their sphere of activity by the shifting of some responsibilities to the regions (*rejony*). This led to the establishment of an internally inconsistent system. Nonetheless the self-government at the lowest local (*gmina*) level has survived. Later, each successive government followed its own, usually different, priorities with respect to the decentralization issue.

Summing up, the significance of competent, non-politicized administration as a contributing factor to a state's stability was not sufficiently appreciated and, consequently, no comprehensive reform program was brought to the implementation stage. The consequences thereof have been very deep demoralization and often glaring incompetence of a substantial part of the administration cadres. A secondary, albeit important, consequence has been a poor quality of policy formulation and implementation in almost every field.

Not only has the substance of institution-building been lagging behind the needs of the state, economy, and society but also the process of law-making left much to be desired. The procedures taken over from the communist times were not based on any particular act regulating the legislative process. There was no link to the Constitution, either. No rules regulated, *inter alia*, the *vacatio legis* principle, no limits were set by the legislature to the delegation of the right to issue regulations by the executive, nor have basic terms and definitions been formulated. This situation has not changed until now. There is no law on how to proceed with the legislative process. Neither have the rules in question been proposed in the Constitution.

Regulations in a period of systemic change are characterized by frequent amendments to both old laws and new, often temporary, rules. There have been some 600 such amendments concerning the economy in the mid-1990s. These hundreds of changes are not the result of the implementation of any coherent program of institutional change concerning the economy. Neither the Sejm nor the executive have been able to ensure the coherence of the law with the requirements of transition. The foregoing is not surprising since no respective bodies, watchdogs of such coherence, have been created. Quite obviously, policy-makers saw no need to even think in such terms.

It would have been impossible, of course, to formulate coherent, stable rules right at the beginning of the transition of the economic system – and in the absence of fundamental institutions, including the absence of a constitution. However, the fact that it was impossible for the new political elite to formulate such a comprehensive program in what has been a very short time-span, and to bring the work on the Constitution to a satisfactory end, should not serve as a justification for the striking inefficiency of the legislative process.

A good example in this respect might be the state of the industrial law (law on business activity). So far, there has been no fundamental act in this field, nor a single judicial register of business firms, where all such entities, regardless of their legal form, would be registered. The process of starting business activity is regulated by the rules contained in 31 different regulations and the fulfillment of the various requirements associated with establishing a firm is time- and resource-consuming. Altogether, the start-up of a registered business, its basic areas of operation, as well as duties of the managers running a firm, are regulated by more than 220 laws which have been passed during the preceding 60 years, and which have been amended approximately 500 times (even excluding the regulations concerning labor law and taxes). Some of these regulations, fundamental for those beginning business activity, have been amended very frequently. For example, in the period under analysis, the Act on Economic Activity of 23 December 1988 (the basic law introducing freedom of business activity) has been amended 11 times (on the average, every 6.5 months), while the Act on Social Insurance has been amended eight times (or once every nine months). This suggests both a low quality of the laws passed during the transition period, as well as a missing sense of direction in the process of systemic change oriented toward greater economic freedom.

Other examples are regulations concerning work safety in registered businesses, which are contained in no less than 120 laws. A number of requirements included there are either inconsistent or unnecessary in a capitalist market economy. Many of them are a dead letter, as it is not possible to enforce them.

An overview of the body of law concerning business activity and the economy in general reveals what amounts to a near-catastrophic situation with respect to its coherence, uniformity, transparency, and even accessibility. A significant part of the law determining duties of economic agents (firms) is found in lower-level regulations issued by various bodies of the executive on the basis of explicit or implicit delegation of the responsibility by the legislature. (Another important matter is whether the legislature has had the right to delegate these responsibilities in the first place!)

The excessively large number of regulations, the frequent amendments following one another in rapid succession, imprecision and incoherence, and sometimes multilevel regulations issued by hierarchies of regulators (the Parliament, the Council of Ministers, and lower-level governmental bodies) make the law unintelligible for non-specialists and impossible to comply with without professional assistance. For small businesses this leads to a significant increase in start-up and operational costs. In sum, the process of systemic change initiated in 1989 has not been supported by improvements in the legislative process.

The quality of law-making has not been supported by the lack of consensus with respect to the fundamentals of the economic system. Often a political orientation reveals its true preferences only through legislative acts. The lack of consistency, already referred to, with respect to the industrial law reflects, among other things, just such a situation. So do the records of many other areas of economic and business legislation.

One such area, concerning territorial self-government (presented in detail by Gilowska 1995, in a paper prepared for this report) is worth a brief mention here. The policy of restoration of local (*gmina* level) self-government undertaken in 1989–90 was full of contradictions and did not constitute a part of any general strategy of decentralization of power within the framework of systemic change. What is more, a restoration of local government was seen more as the fulfillment of an ideological postulate, namely: 'power to the people' (who were disenfranchised by communism) rather than a measure of serious political and economic consequences.

For example, the moment local government was re-established, a new category of property – *municipal* property – was created. According to the law, a significant part of the state property that previously belonged directly to the *gmina* administration and to state enterprises whose so-called founding bodies (direct representatives of the collective owner, that is the state) were these organs of local administration, became municipal property. At the same time, to make things less consistent than they might have been otherwise, municipal ownership has been limited by two developments. First, by the spontaneous *nomenklatura* privatization in the last days of communism, and, second, by the Agricultural Property Agency of the State Treasury. The establishment of the latter deprived the new local self-government bodies of the tax income from land owned by former state farms. Moreover, the activities of the Agency in question have been pursued without regard for the interests of residents of the localities.

Thus, local self-government at the lowest (*gmina*) level has been established but until now it has not been decided within the framework of what system of administration they are going to operate. Their functions and the scope of responsibility have not been unambiguously determined, and a precise division of responsibilities between territorial self-government and central government has not yet been made.

The trend with respect to financing *gmina* activities correlates well with the foregoing. Particularly disturbing is a downward trend in general subsidies as a percentage of the total revenues of *gminas* (from 11.5 percent in 1991 to less than 4 percent in 1994) with a simultaneous increase in the percentage of targeted grants (from 11 percent in 1991 to more than 17 percent in 1994). It is worth noting that the financial resources allocated to *gminas* to fulfill targeted tasks have usually been insufficient and the execution of these tasks has required supplementary financing from *gminas'* own resources. There is a strong conviction among self-government activists that the central government has been trying to establish its control over local self-government through the medium of targeted grants allocated on a discretionary basis.

The above-mentioned ambiguities and political maneuvers are

made easier by the unsolved issue of a clear delineation of respective responsibilities, as well as by the as-yet absent constitutional rules, determining sources of funds of territorial self-government at each level (for even the levels have not yet been decided!).

Overall, we have not yet experienced any increased readiness of political elites and the bureaucracy to transfer a part of their responsibilities and accompanying financial resources to territorial self-government. It has not been well understood that many social tensions could have been defused or at least reduced through decentralization of public administration and the establishment of conflict-resolution mechanisms at the levels closer to the sources of conflicts. The important decentralizing impulses of the 1989–90 period, however haphazard and inconsistent, have had undoubtedly positive effects, but have not been followed in any systematic manner. Worse still, the political change resulting from the 1993 parliamentary elections has severely distorted the process in subsequent years.

These elections brought to power the coalition of two parties with their roots in the communist past – the Alliance of Democratic Left (SLD) and the Polish Peasant Party (PSL). Political rhetoric apart, activists from these two parties are not, and probably never were, communists. But they are not social democrats either. Speaking frankly, these people have hardly been interested in any ideology. For the general aim of staying in power and benefiting therefrom cannot be called an ideology. In practical terms, the SLD and PSL activists in the present coalition are former apparatchiks of the Polish United Workers' Party (PZPR) and the United Peasants' Party (ZSL) and their extensions (the youth, women, cooperative and other organizations). This characteristic feature of a near-complete concentration on career opportunities, without regard for any universal values which are an obstacle in this respect, strongly influences behavioral patterns of these people, when again in power (although in a different, democratic political environment).

Given the foregoing, what vision of a social order, if any, is being pursued by politicians of the present parliamentary majority? We shall try to answer the query not by content analysis of official statements but by analyzing the content of drafts of some important economic regulations which are or have already been 'muddled through' the Sejm by the coalition parties. The term 'muddling through' is used here to describe the situation, when sponsors of a given draft act rapidly and although they use the procedures that are formally consistent with the law, leave little room for normal legislative standards. Thus, experts' opinions, statements of business and professional associations, public hearings – all is done perfunctorily and with blatant disregard for the opinions gathered. The pushing of these regulations through the Parliament is often accompanied by a public disinformation campaign with respect to both the intent of the proposed regulation and the expected results. With party discipline applied to voting on the drafts, they become laws, since the present coalition has the necessary majority to win any non-qualified vote.

The real intentions of the coalition parties may become more transparent, if we look at separate regulations as elements of a puzzle. It is only when we have localized enough elements of a puzzle, they all begin to fall into place, and the shape of a social order preferred by the ex-communist coalition begins to emerge. And, then, we may discover that the emerging system resembles, in important respects, the pre-1989 one (that so many had been trying to leave behind). There are, however, surprisingly few attempts to look at the emerging whole. The main focus even of the opposition parties, the media and the general public is on particular laws rather than on the shape of things to come. Another consequence of this omission is the lack of recognition of the fact that simply through the process of passing ordinary laws, the foundations of a new economic system are being established in Poland (rendering the future Constitution irrelevant in this respect).

Let us have a closer look at one of these laws. The draft of the Act on economic self-government is a document of a particularly misleading nature. It is accompanied by a propaganda campaign that abounds with concealments and distortions. Hence, it is difficult to recognize, in the draft itself, what kind of 'self-government' is being offered to entrepreneurs and other owners. In the draft in question – or, to be more precise, in subsequent drafts of the same law – we read more frequently about the supervision of a 'self-governing' organization over firms that are to be made members on a compulsory basis, about consequences of the non-payment of dues to the organization, or about publishing in the media the decisions of intra-organizational tribunals, than about the activities supporting entrepreneurs' interests.

The draft hardly refers to grassroots control over the functioning of the said 'self-governing' organization. Thus, for example, there is no right of appeal to the ordinary courts against the decisions of the organization's internal tribunals. The Act infringes upon the principles of democratic choice by giving the executive, i.e. the organization's bureaucracy, the authority to limit both the active and passive voting rights of members. Also, it limits members' influence on the performance of the 'self-governing' organization's bureaucracy and the established internal tribunals. With respect to the latter, the draft does not determine the substantive rules and procedure of these tribunals. Significantly, the right to do so is delegated to the central bureaucracy of this peculiar 'self-governing' body.

Thus, an 'economic self-government' (as it is called) is being created, over which neither its (compulsorily drafted) members, nor the judiciary, and the general public have much control. However, a meticulous care has been taken of this organization's revenues in the form of compulsory contributions (to be established in a typical discretionary fashion, that is, without specifying their value, even in relative terms, for example, as a fraction of a turnover of a member firm). Characteristically, in this single case, the role of general judicial and administrative procedures has been invoked because unpaid dues will be, according to the draft, exacted from members in arrears in accordance with the proceedings applied to collection of unpaid taxes.

Under any accepted interpretation, the establishment of a self-government, territorial or other, implies a limitation of the state administration's responsibilities that are – in a given area of responsibility – taken over by a self-government authority. It exercises its own rights and fulfills its own duties, which are not conferred upon the self-governing bodies by orders of the state administration. But in the case of this peculiar 'self-governing' organization, it is designed in a manner allowing it first of all to implement tasks ordered by the state and, consequently, to discipline its compulsory members on behalf of the state.

Summing up, the draft of the law in question undermines the principles of democracy, the principles of a *Rechtstaat*, and the basic features of a market economy. It is, however, well correlated with a vision of a system, without mechanisms of grassroots control over the exercise of power by elected authorities. Its inspiration comes from the well known Leninist idea of organizations as 'conveyor belts' from the political vanguard to the masses. The ghost of 'democratic centralism' hovers above 'economic self-government'.

Other drafts or laws that have already been 'muddled through' the parliament display many similar characteristics. What particularly strikes analysts is the extent of regulatory powers delegated to the executive. The scope and extent is so unjustifiably large as to jeopardize the traditional continental tripartite division between the legislature, executive, and judiciary – at the expense of the legislative authorities.

Finally, it is impossible not to look at the process of writing the future Constitution. The fundamental feature – agreed upon in principle – is that the *Rechtstaat* guarantees the equality of rights and that their differentiation and limitations take place exclusively on the basis of acts of the legislature. These principles of the *Rechtstaat* are not, however, observed in the rule-making practice, given the unjustifiable scope and extent of the delegation of the regulatory power to the executive. Another dubious practice, already stressed here, is the tactic of the post-communist coalition to decide about important characteristics of the economic system through a series of ordinary acts of parliament – ahead of the choices made in these respects in the future constitution.

There is more than a lingering suspicion that the ruling coalition appears to assume that a future constitution will constitute the mere facade that will accommodate any system, political and economic. The ex-communists do not seem to be concerned with such 'details' as the question whether the Constitution will decide about decentralization or centralization of the state, whether it will weaken or strengthen the position of the executive, or whether it will limit the role of the state in the economy or, contrarily, will allow direct control over economic activity.

It should be noted that, historically, the stimulus to enacting a constitution has been – with totalitarian exceptions – the need to limit the power of the state. But in post-communist Poland, according to the draft constitution being prepared at present, this does not seem to be the case. The emerging draft does not strongly protect the rights of the people as it leaves the executive a near-complete freedom in expanding both the scope and extent of its rule-making power. Under such circumstances the emerging constitution will become little more than a facade.

And, yet, the constitution is normally the product of a society that has decided to organize its state in a way that ensures the members of that society their freedoms. These freedoms are formulated as fundamental principles and protected by a given constitution. The constitution, then, ensures that the state acts in ways that are in concordance with society's preferences expressed in the constitutional act. This is the origin of the law-state (the *Rechtstaat*), in which even a parliamentary majority is not allowed to disregard constitutional principles. Normally, the constitution is not a collection of catch phrases, or declarations of intentions; it is a very precise list of fundamental principles guaranteeing freedoms of the citizens and precise delineation of functions and powers of the state authorities.

Unfortunately, it is a declaratory 'manifesto' that is likely to emerge from the Polish parliament and, as such, unable to effectively ensure the protection of freedoms. The stream of catch phrases substitutes for the guarantees of most fundamental economic freedoms: the freedom to pursue chosen economic activity, the freedom to manage and dispose of one's property, the protection of professional and trade secrets, the limitations of arbitrariness of the state in setting taxes, etc. Also missing are the principles of the responsibility of the state for activities (both acts of commission and omission) of its executive bodies and the corresponding rights of citizens to just compensation for damages resulting from such activities.

Altogether it may be said with conviction, based on the analysis of a large number of drafts submitted to the Parliament by the executive apparatus of the ruling SLD/PSL coalition, that the overriding concept is that of a vast corporatist state, an unremitting growth of the discretionary power of state bureaucracy, and the creation of quasi-public institutions serving the particular interest groups within the coalition (first of all the apparatchiks of the ex-communist parties) in ways that conflict with the acceptable budgetary standards of the civilized state.

A particularly important area of the well-functioning *Rechtstaat* is the sphere of the interaction of private interests and public administration. Here, the rules should be particularly precise to allow for necessary oversight and minimization of the potential for corruption. A closer look at a substantial number of proposed drafts gives the impression that the opposite is the case. Rules, both those already passed by the Parliament and those at the drafting stage, have been formulated in such a manner as to create the opportunity for bureaucrats and others associated with the ruling coalition to draw benefits, often legally, from the created institutions through their governing rules specially designed for the purpose. It is difficult to underestimate the threat posed by the foregoing for the

Polish state. Corruption in the sphere of implementation of the law is corrosive in the long run, as an Italian example indicates. However, corruption in the sphere of law-making is akin to a time bomb being planted underneath a given state.

3

THE FINANCIAL MARKETS
Underdeveloped rather than distorted
Jan Winiecki

For many reasons the development of financial markets has lagged behind that of goods markets. The development, noted already elsewhere (see, for example, *PPRG Report* 1993), has had its sources, however, not so much in the neglect of financial markets by the transition-oriented governments of the 1989–93 period but in the nature of financial markets. For financial markets require both organizationally-intensive regulation (in the sense of Levy 1993) and the emergence of private economic agents specializing in financial services.

To begin with the first requirement, Levy distinguishes two types of institutional changes. One is what he calls *stroke-of-a-pen measures* that change the rules of the game by freeing economic agents from the shackles of restraints such as price liberalization, or abolition of exchange controls, another is *organizationally-intensive measures*, elaborated regulations that lay the groundwork for the operations of markets or authorities in their interaction with economic agents, such as stock exchange regulations, tax code, etc.

In the case of Poland and other ex-communist countries the organizationally-intensive regulatory process has to go hand-in-hand with the emergence of private economic agents: both those specializing in financial markets' services and the users of these services. To give but one simple example: the stock market developments are not only dependent on the political climate conducive to its creation and further development and, subsequently, on the elaboration of rules and the emergence of respective organizations applying these rules, but also on the emergence of capitalists, whether of the owner-manager or corporate variety. Thus, for example, privatization must be seen as a process closely intertwined with the development of capital markets (a point elaborated in a special paper for this report, see Hockuba 1995).

The foregoing does not mean that there has been no neglect on the part of policy-makers. There was, first of all, a rather weak understanding of the importance of the disindebtment issue (i.e. of getting rid of a debt inherited by state enterprises from the communist past of financial irresponsibility). This became a serious issue only late in 1991 (see the letter of the advisors of the Prime Minister to the Polish President, Beksiak et al. 1991). Also, there has been a lack of clear-cut strategy with respect to some markets, compounded by an inability to differentiate between what is desirable and what is attainable. Nonetheless it may be said that, on the whole, financial markets have been more underdeveloped than distorted (the way labor markets in Poland are, as shown in Chapter 4). Of course, different pillars of the financial system are in different stages of development. The longest existing, most developed has been the banking system.

The Polish financial system has been from the start of transition, dependent on commercial banks. Commercial banking has the longest track record and partly due to its (relatively) long existence has accumulated the largest dose of distortions. Regional commercial banks had already been separated from the old communist monobank in late 1988 and, after seven years in operation, still enjoyed, together with three old state-owned specialized banks, an overwhelming majority of total credit creation. Small, generally undercapitalized, private banks have been unable to dislodge the large SOEs from their dominant position as has happened in quite a few sectors of the Polish economy. The reason for this has been largely an ambivalent policy toward foreign investment in the commercial banking sector. The Finance Ministry, which is responsible for privatization, has been first, afraid of the criticism from both Left and Right and therefore did not look any too energetically for potential core investors in Polish commercial banks. Later, the ex-communist coalition became even less forthcoming and disregarded the interest of those few investors that were already there. At the same time, the central bank (NBP), which is in charge of the concessions to open new banks, has been very parsimonious with the granting of such concessions and has encouraged foreign banks to take over small private banks in trouble as an 'entry price' to the Polish commercial banking market. As a result, there are a few subsidiaries of large foreign banks in Poland and none, with maybe the exception of the Dutch group ING, has won a noticeable share in aggregate credit creation. This is in stark contrast to Hungary, where foreign commercial banks, on their own or in joint-ventures with domestic banks, hold more than one third of the total commercial bank assets.

Apart from the attitude toward foreign investment, there has been throughout, a similar ambivalence to the kind of banking system Poland should aim at. Many experts tend to suggest that the best choice is the Anglo-Saxon model of banking, where capital markets are the paramount means of acquiring new resources, enforcing market discipline over the performance of firms, and resolving conflicts between owners and managers. Others prefer the German/Japanese model of financial/industrial groups or, at the very least, banks' shareholding in industrial firms, where discipline and managerial control conflicts are resolved without external, that is the capital market, intervention.

These preferences have been stated, often by policy-makers themselves, without regard to two crucial determinants of the development of the banking system:

1 They do not take into account an important difference between the desirability and *attainability* of the particular model under the time and place-specific conditions of post-communist transition. Poland is not an exception here, by the way. Thus, although the present writer is in agreement with many experts as to the desirability of the Anglo-Saxon model, with its pivotal role of the capital markets and the clear division of functions between commercial (or retail) banking and investment (or merchant) banking, he is skeptical about the attainability of this model in the foreseeable future.

   Developments in Poland push the banking system in the opposite direction. A variety of measures, including the legislated debt-reduction procedure of 1993, push banks in the direction of shareholding in non-financial firms. So far they have been strikingly reluctant to convert debt into equity. But the investment requirements of restructured SOEs or already privatized SOEs will undoubtedly increase the pressure. Therefore, the probability of ending up with the German/Japanese model of universal banks – holding shares and exercising control over a significant share of the non-financial sector – seems to be markedly higher.

2 The fact that alternative models referred to above are not clear-cut alternatives nowadays, is not taken into account. There is a

noticeable blurring of the lines in the countries of origin of the German/Japanese model, especially in the former. The awakening of German shareholders who increasingly cease to be passive observers of the decisions taken without their consent (let alone participation), combined with the increased securitization of financial instruments used by the non-financial sector, tend to increase the role of capital markets and their control over the performance of firms. The internationalization of banking and the stronger role of investment banking, are also supportive of the tendency in question. Therefore, one may expect that in East-Central and Eastern Europe also the evolution of the banking system will be in the longer-run shifting toward the 'mixed' model, with the increasing role of institutions of the capital markets.

It is against such a – more realistic – perspective that one should set the frame for further development of the Polish commercial banking sector. A clear priority here should be the privatization of all state-owned commercial banks. But it is here that the most distortive and disquieting developments have taken place since 1993.

First of all, privatization of the state-owned commercial banks has proceeded slowly, reluctantly – and increasingly acrimoniously. To begin with, by the end of 1995, only four out of nine regional banks spun off the old communist monobank had been privatized (and none of the separately existing state banks). Moreover, it has been noted already (Kostrzewa 1994) their privatization has been more a nominal than real phenomenon. For whenever the Treasury owns the largest package of shares, usually between 30 and 40 percent, the actual decision-making process is heavily influenced if not actually determined by the Finance Ministry. The road to real-life privatization depends largely on the ownership structure. And, with the noted reluctance of the authorities to allow foreign banks to become core shareholders, this road will be long (if there is no opening up of the banking sector under the provisions of the European Union accession treaty – see below).

The continuous dominant influence of politics over the lending policies of nominally privatized commercial banks has been warmly embraced by the ex-communist coalition. Since the parties in question are allied first and foremost by their desire to maximize benefits from their being in power through both political favoritism (necessary to remain in power) and personal enrichment (as a goal *per se*), they not only maintained influence over the privatized banks but went much further in that direction. A government concept, put forward in late 1994, of a banking sector consolidation without privatization ostensibly has the aim of strengthening the banking sector by making it more competitive through enforced mergers. However, there are serious doubts about both ends and means of such an intervention in the commercial banking sectors. As far as ends are concerned, there is a strong and well substantiated suspicion that ostensible aims are not the most important ones. First, it is suspected, given the record of this coalition, that the consolidated banks will be used as a vehicle for an increase in central control over the economy and for the dispensation of the 'goodies' of political favoritism. The dominant state role, even after the nominal privatization, will ensure, as stressed for example by Zieliński (1994), that the consolidated banks will finance ruling coalition pet projects, more often than not propping up perennial state-owned loss-makers with the aim of supporting ex-communists' political clientele.

It should be noted that the consolidation without privatization (or with later apparent rather than real privatization) fits very well into the more general pattern of institutional and policy measures undertaken or aimed at by the ruling coalition. Thus, a law on commercialization and privatization of SOEs that provides for commercialization for different purposes than privatization, aims quite clearly at maintaining as large a state sector as possible for the twin purposes of political favoritism and personal enrichment (more about that particular development in Chapter 5). Besides, the weakness of the ostensible argumentation is shown by the experience of Western banks, where larger projects related to infrastructural investment and financial restructuring of large non-financial corporations are not financed by individual banks, however large they may be (and there would be hundreds of Western banks larger than Polish banks even after consolidation). Even the best prepared projects within the financial capacity of these large banks are nonetheless financed by consortia because prudent internal rules do not allow banks to concentrate risk to such an extent [see 'Poland', OECD, 1995]. Therefore, the suspicion that the state-controlled banks will be used to finance loss-makers that would be evaluated as unfit for large loans by any efficiency criteria, is made stronger.

Moreover, one should remind the reader about the dicta of theory of dispersed knowledge and property rights' theory. First, the amalgamation by bureaucratic fiat (government-managed consolidation) is an inferior solution due to the fact that knowledge is dispersed (and partly inarticulate) and, consequently, bureaucratic decisions will be made on the basis of much less knowledge than that of the interested parties (if they found it in their interest to amalgamate). And, second, decisions taken by those who do not bear the financial cost of failure are also going to be inferior because of the question of moral hazard: here, the willingness to take greater risk than acceptable by those who bear such consequences. Therefore, privatization should precede any voluntary consolidation that may be taken by the interested parties in the future.

The present government, however, has persisted in its theoretically erroneous (but opportunistically perceived to be beneficial) approach. Worse still, in its eagerness to get the aforementioned benefits of consolidated state banks, it has been ready to disregard, not only sound economics, but even the law. For the consolidation proposal of early 1996 included into consolidated groups banks that have already been privatized and had a majority of their shares in private hands. Thus, foreign and domestic shareholders could have woken up one day to find themselves in *de facto* nationalized banks! Moreover, such an operation (i.e. automatic consolidation) which, according to the proposal in question, would have proceeded without proper valuation of new shares, or credible audits would engender a variety of risks (differentiated loan portfolios of different amalgamated banks, differing investment patterns, etc.) for present shareholders. Normally they are protected against such risk by the respective provisions of the commercial code (Stefanowicz 1996).

The outcry the proposal generated, including interventions by some foreign shareholders, as well as less visible enquiries of international financial institutions (one of which, the EBRD (European Bank for Reconstruction and Development), is a substantial shareholder in some earlier privatized banks), made the government retract its original plan to include in the consolidation program those banks that had already been privatized. The problem remains, though. The government's intention to create pliable instruments of financing politically-expedient but economically-unjustified projects, through consolidation of state-owned banks, made the development of the Polish banking system look even less predictable, the Polish government look even less welcoming for potential foreign investors, and last but not least, made the probability of the emergence of well-capitalized joint-ventures of privatized state banks with major foreign banks even less likely. This possibility, in particular, should be regarded as a major failure, for it has been for years the most important aim of architects of Polish transition. An urge to live off the state, coupled with the arrogance of the ruling *apparatchiki* and their striking inability to predict consequences of their own actions, strongly undermined efforts of earlier non-communist governments.

The whole consolidation program has been not only ill-conceived in terms of its ostensible (rather than real) aims but it is also ill-timed. As stressed by representatives of the banking community, an amalgamation of a few banks into a reasonably well-performing unit needs time – and a lot of it. From this vantage point the whole consolidation program definitely comes too late. In 1997 Poland has to open its market to European Union-based banks and therefore such amalgamation would throw the consolidated banks into a disarray that would undermine the ability of Polish state-owned banks to compete, which is not particularly good as it is.

The concentration on the consolidation issue has, moreover, interfered with the need to further improve the functioning of the banking system as a whole. Thus, although there has been progress noted on prudential issues the whole system of deposit insurance has not yet begun to function. Among aspects of banking activity that are still not performing one should also mention the payment (clearing) system. Moreover, left half-solved – and in an unsatisfactory manner at that – has been restructuring of some major state-owned banks, especially that of the hybrid state–cooperative banking structure headed by the Bank for Food Economy (BGŻ). Here again, the centralization drive, associated with the wish to use the BGŻ as both a well-paid workplace for the *apparatchiki* from the rural satellite of the communist party, and a source of not-necessarily-to-be-repaid loans for the privileged (a well-known BGŻ feature even from the most recent past), triumphed over the economic sense. Similar is the prospect of the former savings monobank (PKO BP), the one that held the monopoly for the population's savings, with its bloated portfolio of housing loans.

Next, we should have a look at the Polish stock exchange which has been the first component of capital markets to emerge. Foreign experts generally stress the competence with which the institutional framework of the Polish stock exchange has been set up (see, e.g., 'Poland', OECD, 1995). Also, the choice of the arrangements well suited for the needs of the small market with low liquidity has been the right one. However, the market for years has been excessively small. Although its capitalization increased since 1991 to about 4 percent of GDP by the mid-1990s (Hockuba 1995), nonetheless Warsaw Stock Exchange (WSE) is still closer in its size to Dhaka Stock Exchange in Bangladesh (market value of shares up to 1 percent of GDP) than to some other emerging stock exchanges of, say, Thailand (78 percent of GDP) or Korea (101 percent of GDP). The foregoing has largely been the result of the dramatically small supply of firms suitable for listing on the stock exchange. And this, in turn, reflected an uneven and generally not very rapid rate of privatization. For it should be kept in mind that it is privatized rather than generic private firms that may successfully fulfil the criteria, especially those of the minimum size in the first five or, maybe, even 10 years of transition. Therefore, at the start of 1994 there were only 24 firms listed on the first tier, with 19 of them being privatized firms. Only one firm has been listed on the second tier. In March 1996 there were 57 firms listed on the first and 15 listed on the second tier (altogether 72 firms); still not very impressive numbers. This will not change at any time soon, as stressed already in the overview and again, in Chapter 5, because of the well-known resistance to, and distaste for, privatization on the side of the dominant part of the ruling coalition.

The problems are, however, manifold, even if we exclude those stemming from the small size of the stock exchange. First and foremost, the stock market did not play the role for which it has been established in the first place. After all, capital markets exist to provide long-term financing for start-up and expanding enterprises. Financing is obtained by selling equity in the firm or by issuing debt instruments (typically bonds). In the case of the stock exchange it is securities that are sold through public offering. However, in Poland, the public offerings of firms appearing on the WSE have not been the means of long-term financing but the source of revenue to the Treasury. It is only with the fourth year of WSE existence that the first capital increases and other issues of the already listed firms have taken place. Still, the amount of new capital raised on the Warsaw Stock Exchange is minuscule compared with other sources of financing.

Another problem that revealed its greater urgency of late is the role of the state on the stock exchange and/or *vis-à-vis* listed firms in which it remains a major shareholder. Raiffeisen Capital & Investment, a brokerage firm, has collected data on 20 major institutional shareholders, according to the value of share prices on 2 June 1995 (*Gazeta Wyborcza*, 7 June 1995). According to their calculations, the Treasury was a major shareholder exceeding by far any other, with a share in the total capitalization of the WSE of 15.8 percent, way ahead of the next four shareholders: PepsiCo, ING Group, the EBRD, and Heineken, who, except for the EBRD, only held shares in companies in which they were the sole or major shareholders. The first professional investment fund, actively participating in the market, the PIONEER, was sixth with 1.4 percent of the total. However, apart from the Treasury, certain other state agencies were also shareholders, the largest of them being the Agency for Economic Development (ARG – Agencja Rozwoju Gospodarczego), with 0.8 percent of the WSE capitalization.

Although state agencies, including the Treasury, have not been very active traders, their potential for distortionary behavior is quite considerable. In 1994 and early 1995, the case for tightening the rules of public agencies' behavior on the stock market was made by the careless behavior and incompetent management of the ARG that actively traded, without specific authorization and without competence, on the stock exchange, incurring substantial losses. (Characteristically for the 'cronies-stick-together' type of attitude of the ex-communists, nothing happened after the fact has been revealed by the Press.)

However, the recent behavior of the government in announcing, as noted already, the amalgamation of state-owned banks with banks that were already privatized and listed on the stock exchange (in which the Treasury held large packages of shares) put the danger of state behavior on the stock exchange into a sharper focus.

The most obvious answer to the problem seems to be state divestment, preferably mandated by law. However, the intentions of the ruling coalition seem to be moving in the opposite direction, increasing the potential for harmful intervention (quite apart from the potential for corruption). The subsequent drafts of the law on the state Treasury invariably empower various agencies, acting as Treasury agents, to trade in shares on the stock exchange.

Thus, the potential for distortions, or maybe even for hidden renationalization is expected to increase rather than decrease under the present political circumstances. The transgressions against the capitalist market order are so serious in this respect that the Freedom Union (that is the main opposition party)'s legal experts proposed the constitutional ban on 'stock market-based renationalization'. This, however, like the acceleration of privatization, looks to be a legislative task for the future rather than for the present.

There is one more drawback resulting from the relatively small share of active institutional investors on the stock exchange, namely, the exceedingly large influence of individual investors and their investment decisions. Without an increase in the number of active institutional investors, and an increase in their share of the total capitalization, the Warsaw Stock Exchange will be prone to much larger price fluctuations than would have been possible otherwise – even at the present level of the capitalization of the WSE.

Investment funds of various types have been rather slow in appearing on Polish capital markets. This has been partly due to the normal problems of newly liberalized economies treated as high-risk territory for potential foreign investors (see, *i.a.*, Winiecki 1995b) and partly due to the *ab*normal level of bureaucratic *un*coordination (and often resistance), characteristic of Polish transition. Also, over time, one obstacle was the lack of regulations concerning closed-end investment funds (a draft of the relevant regulation was only completed in the Ministry for Ownership Transformation by the mid-1990s).

Certainly the largest group of investment funds to have appeared on the Polish capital markets has been National Investment Funds involved in the Polish Mass Privatization Program (PPP) – some four hundred within the 10 years time-span. The PPP started in 1996, with five years' delay, and this may be regarded as a sign of change for the better, but the restructuring and privatizing seems to be a long way off. The long story of the PPP is certainly worth telling and the advantages and disadvantages of the program worth analyzing (see, *i.a.*, Winiecki's 1995 paper specially prepared for this report) but in this section it is enough to point out that, given the narrowly circumscribed mandate of NIFs, their active role on capital markets outside the area of privatization of SOEs in their portfolios seems – at present at least – rather unlikely. As for other, traditionally-found investment funds, some of them, such as pension funds, have no market worth talking about before serious reform of the social security system has taken place. Some others are emerging one by one, although at a less-than-satisfactory rate, given the needs of the rapidly expanding generic private sector in the transition economy, but more in accordance with the normal sequence of foreign investment in the liberalizing economy.

Probably the most pressing need is that of venture capital for the private small business sector. Since it is well known that small and medium sized firms everywhere, not only in post-communist economies in transition, have much more circumscribed access to loan capital, the availability of high-risk equity capital is a highly desirable and wealth-increasing factor. An increase in the supply of loan and equity capital for the private small business sector is probably the only one area of financial markets, where the direct role of the state, if played in a judicious, market-enhancing manner, may reduce the risk level for private bankers and investors.

While considering financial markets, it is worth stressing that healthy development of these markets is dependent not only on the institutional framework for financial markets *per se* but also on the supportive political, legal, and economic environments. To quote two experts on the subject:

> laws, regulations, and economic policies that encourage the expansion of private enterprises also contribute to the development of capital and equity markets because they increase demand for long-term finance. The legal framework, economic policy, private sector growth, and capital mobilization, therefore, are interrelated.
>
> (Painter and Rourke 1993: 248)

Seen from this vantage point, Polish financial (not only capital) markets cannot be said to enjoy a particularly conducive environment, especially of late. First of all, the slow privatization process reduces the supply of large private firms and this characteristic has been typical since the beginning of Polish privatization. Second, and in the longer run more important, the generic private sector has been increasingly affected of late by the rising depth and extent of intrusive state regulation. The burden of the already introduced and/ or forthcoming regulation will unavoidably reduce flexibility, innovativeness, and generally entrepreneurship. This, in turn, will adversely affect profitability – and, in consequence, these firms' standing on financial markets. Relatively low level of supply and at the same time reduced level of demand by more slowly expanding firms may create a situation known as a low-level equilibrium. In plain words it means underdeveloped financial markets even in the longer run, and this threatens the healthy development of the Polish economy.

It must be emphasized that what has been pointed out so far, however important, is only one barrier to the development of financial markets (and, therefore, the national economy). There are many others as well. In view of the foregoing, the recommendations concerning financial markets formulated below contain proposals both aimed at the improved performance of financial markets and a better environment for that improved performance:

1 With respect to the banking sector the primary task for the near future is the rapid privatization of the remaining state banks and the divestment of the Treasury from substantial shareholdings in the already privatized commercial banks. For the medium-term the issue of consolidation with the aim of increased economies of scale of Polish banks should be left to the market. The government should refrain from raising obstacles if such consolidation involves one or more large foreign banks that are expected to enter the Polish banking sector as of 1997, that is, when EU-domiciled banks become free to enter the country's banking sector. It is generally recognized, both among analysts and within the banking community, that the capital base of most Polish banks is highly inadequate and a substantial part of the capital to remedy this deficiency has to come from abroad. Thus, a substantial part of the consolidation will be led by foreign banks.

2 Rapid privatization is also necessary to strengthen the resolve of privatized banks in resisting political pressures to support uncreditworthy clients (usually SOEs) and financially non-viable projects (usually put together within the public sector). Private banks with a stronger ownership control over the management are far less likely to get involved in financially unsound, blatantly political support of state firms and state-sponsored projects.

3 In view of the tendency to create a variety of state agencies (Treasury agents authorized to operate on the stock market, other agencies, including those *in statu nascendi*, who are authorized to operate on goods and factor markets), the recommendation is that such activities are very precisely defined in their aims and procedures so that they are not allowed to lead to renationalizations through market means.

4 Even the privatization and market-led consolidation of the Polish commercial banking sector will not solve the problem of large infrastructural projects, that require involvement of a variety of private consortia operating in the flexible and yet predictable legal-financial environment. Infrastructural sectors increasingly

turn to foreign private investors for financing. Also, such consortia function generally on non-recourse basis (without state guarantees). So far it is only in telecommunications that the process of involvement has been put into operation (although, unfortunately, accompanied by the atmosphere of scandal and litigation that may have deleterious effects on foreign investors' involvement in other sectors). The conducive environment should be established for a variety of financial arrangements, especially of the BOT (build–operate–transfer) type. It should be kept in mind, as it was put frankly at a conference on financing the Polish energy sector, that many countries aggressively court private investors, guaranteeing them rates of return that are sufficiently attractive to warrant consideration. If we do not offer both a conducive regulatory framework and the sort of economic opportunities that are offered elsewhere, the inflow of capital to infrastructural projects in the energy sector, road system, and so on, will never reach a significant size.

5 As far as the general rules of the environment for the financial markets is concerned, what is necessary is a stable tax system that does not discriminate against some forms of saving and investment. This is what is now looming large over the stock exchange: the tax on capital gains from transactions in securities and short-term money market instruments. However, the capital gains tax will create a well-known problem of privileging the least active form of saving, that is bank savings (as interest income is not taxed). Although there are good reasons for not taxing any gains from savings (the income they come from has already been taxed), at a minimum we recommend a uniform – and low – level of taxation of all gains from saving. Moreover, to encourage long-term saving, income from investment instruments maintained for more than, say, six or 12 months should be free from any taxation (a former president of the Polish Development Bank prefers six months, see Kostrzewa 1994).

There are also other drawbacks of the present stock market arrangements but probably not as disturbing as those outlined above. They are analyzed competently elsewhere (see *PPRG Report* 1993).

Almost non-existent on the Polish financial scene are non-banking financial institutions, such as investment funds, trust funds and pension funds, which convert savings into investments without endangering the macroeconomic stability. Their presence enormously broadens the scope of capital markets. However, for this presence to materialize certain conditions must be fulfilled. The regulatory framework must be set, the Polish Mass Privatization Program (PPP) must at last be put into operation. This will put some 15–20 new players, i.e. investment funds, on the market. Finally, there must be a definite political will to decide on the fundamentals of the social security system and the role of private pension funds therein (plus the necessary regulatory framework for such funds). Of these probably the closest to implementation is the PPP and the appearance on the scene of investment funds as stockholders in companies included in the program (this has already happened). The pros and cons of this solution have been debated for quite some time and there is no need to repeat them here (the present writer has evaluated the program, see Winiecki's 1995 paper specially prepared for this report). It should be stressed at this point that regardless of criticism, it is better to privatize in a less satisfactory manner than not to privatize at all. And better still if the new capital market players that emerge as a result are allowed to broaden the scope of their activities so as to add to the extremely thin layer of agents acting on the capital markets.

Now, although the fundamentals, or the Hayekian 'general rules', were considered in Chapter 2, the sound development of the financial markets requires not a few specific legal arrangements, apart from the general commercial and civil codes, enhancing the certainty of contractual relations and reducing transaction costs. The Polish set of rules strengthening the financial markets is far from complete. For example, the most adverse effects are the non-existence of laws on secured lending on the ability of businesses, especially smaller and medium-sized ones to raise loans. At present there are neither the rules nor a register, from where a potential lender(s) may learn whether the specific collateral proposed by a given borrower is free from earlier security interest (or lien). This situation is, most probably, a greater deterrent to lending than the near non-existent system of guarantees designed as an incentive for lenders to take a risk in lending to borrowers with a less than ironclad track record (usually smaller and newer business entities).

The law on secured lending may be the most urgently needed, but experts in the field see also the need for modification of some of the existing laws. A prime candidate for such procedure is the law on bankruptcy. There, the (typical) over-privileged position of the state and its agencies (treasury, state social security) is so overwhelming that it became a serious obstacle undermining the role of bankruptcy in the Polish economy. The legislated priority of the state to all real estate, movables and receivables goes so far as to even give the state priority over the legal costs of bankruptcy proceedings themselves. Therefore courts often decide against instituting bankruptcy because they are not able to find the means of satisfying their own claim arising out of the bankruptcy procedure (see Płoch 1995). Altogether, the legal environment is still more a hindrance than a prop-up for the financial markets, adding to the uncertainties stemming from past mistakes and adverse political currents.

4

THE LABOR MARKET
Distorted rather than underdeveloped
Jan Winiecki

The Polish labor market is characterized by severe distortions and these distortions cannot be explained solely by the distortionary legacy of its communist past. New layers of distortions have been added by the *de facto* political balance of power which has evolved in Poland since the beginning of political change. Thus, the basic problem of the labor market is a very unequal balance of rights and obligations between labor and capital in the Polish economy in favor of the former. More apparent than real under the communist system (in spite of the slogans of the 'leading role' of the working class), it has gained in importance since 1989, with the ascendancy of a 'Solidarity'-based coalition with its strong beliefs in workers' self-management. It is worth reminding readers that the historical round-table confirmed – at the insistence of 'Solidarity' – the important rights of employees' representation.

As stressed in a special paper prepared for this report (Mickiewicz 1995), the new strength of employees' representation definitely changed the balance of power in state-owned enterprises (whether later privatized or not). A good indicator of the power of labor are decisions that normally are exercised by owners, that is management changes. From September 1989 to March 1992 new managers were appointed in 86 percent of all SOEs subordinated (formally) to the Ministry of Industry. In over three-quarters of cases (76.6 percent) previous managers have been recalled at the initiative of trade unions or employee self-management councils. The year 1989 may, then, be seen as a dividing line and the beginning of the new distribution of property rights in state enterprises (regardless of their legal form).

Property rights theory is clear on this point: the right to choose management and the right to the residual income are fundamental rights of ownership. Therefore, it should also be noted that the behavior of unions and/or self-management councils concerning the residual income (i.e. profit) of these *de facto* employee-owned enterprises has been no less injurious to the rights of the owner (i.e. the state). The strategy of increasing wages in order to leave as little profit as possible for further distribution has been only to some limited extent countervailed by wage controls in the form of a tax-based incomes policy (one of the so-called 'anchors' of the stabilization program) and an asset tax (taxes were, misleadingly, called dividends).

The unequal balance of power has continued to exert its influence on the labor market and beyond throughout the whole post-1989 period. Labor's position remained dominant under both the Polish non-communist governments and the ex-communist governments. The main reason is that both major political groupings have strong links to organized labor: the non-communist coalition that led Poland in 1989–93, with their links to Solidarity, and the ex-communists after 1993, with their links to the former official communist trade union (OPZZ).

It was the political imbalance in favor of factor labor that led subsequent governments to tolerate the delays in the tax payment or outright non-payment by a large number of SOEs. The story has been the same with respect to the payment of social security contributions. The political nature of such forgiveness will become all the clearer as we point out the fact that it has been positively correlated with the size of delinquent enterprises. It should also be noted that in a number of cases, this forgiveness contravened the law. For the law clearly states that the declaration of bankruptcy is obligatory in those cases where the total debt exceeds the asset value of the firm.

The political imbalance generally led governments toward corporatist models. Mrs Suchocka's government sought the idea of a 'social pact' that was to be negotiated with trade unions as a price for social peace. The ex-communist coalition did not suggest anything formal but in many pronouncements stressed a negotiating model of trilateral relations (government–trade union–business organizations). The foregoing suggests the weak position of post-1989 governments (see Flanagan 1991, quoted in Mickiewicz 1996) as they assumed that they might lower political risk by shifting a share of responsibility for failure onto other partners in the negotiations.

One may, however, ask a question: if trade unions have been unusually strong, why were employers' organizations by contrast so weak? Part of the answer is, of course, historical. Trade unions were already there, when democracy arrived (even Solidarity had existed *de facto* for almost a decade). Employers' associations have been, without doubt, a new phenomenon, without any experience in recruitment and organization. Moreover, employers in the many organizations that cropped up in Poland were a mixed lot. It also meant people who were in no way employers in the strict sense of the word. For these organizations covered only a few private owners–entrepreneurs (usually owners of large firms) and much more numerous managers of state enterprises, with no ownership stake at all. Moreover, the overwhelming majority of employers, owners of small and medium-sized businesses, do not belong to any organization. In their everyday struggle for survival and growth they do not yet appreciate well enough the benefits of speaking with amplified voice, resulting from speaking in the name of large numbers of other business people having the same interests. Therefore, in numerical terms, they are no match for trade unions. And in politics it is large numbers that matter. If politicians have the choice between supporting the case of a few dozen entrepreneurs and tens of thousands of employees mobilized (or potentially mobilized) by trade unions, more often than not they tilt toward the position of the latter – and regardless of the merits of the case at that. They clearly know where the votes are. The issue has been presented at the Polish Business Council by Winiecki (1993a).

To give an example, there are in Poland probably a quarter of a million of employees engaged in firms and unincorporated, self-employed individuals involved in the import, production and distribution (wholesale and retail) of clothing. Had they been organized in, say, a clothing section of some employers' association, they would certainly be heard if they protested, for example, against the protectionist demands of the declining and inefficient state textile and clothing enterprises. Politicians, however inept, can at least count, and succumbing to the protectionist sentiments of the latter would mean creating hostility in a quarter of a million potential voters (in fact: many more, as families should often be counted as well). Building coalitions of that sort is a resource-consuming and time-consuming activity, but given the unique Polish political and social scene it is undoubtedly preferable to doing nothing and leaving the political field to the economic forces of yesterday.

The example used here reveals also another feature of Polish transition, namely an imbalance between the political representation of the state enterprise sector and private business sector. Although the latter is very large, comprising 8 million employers and employees, it is a political midget, compared to the former. Given the strong influence of unions on both major political camps, the political clout of the state sector is disproportionally greater, with the private sector outside agriculture having almost no say in both the institution-building process and actual economic policies.

The labor code with its continuous stream of amendments, uniformly in favor of labor, is a good example of both the unequal power balance between labor and capital and between the state enterprise and private business sector. For it is only in the private sector that owners bear the cost of labor code provisions in favor of the employees. In the case of the state enterprise sector, with its 'soft' budget constraint, these costs are shifted on the state, that is the taxpayers, either through lower profits or open or disguised subsidies of state enterprises.

The unequal status of both parties of the industrial relations is best exemplified by the existence of the right of employees to strike but the non-existence of the right of employers to lock-out (even as a defensive measure, i.e. in response to a strike). Polish labor code abounds in provisions that do not appear in respective labor codes of market economies, even the excessively regulated and 'welfarized' ones, such as, for example, paragraph 13 requiring that employers and the state 'should try to ensure the decent reward for work'. Thus, the economic meaning of wage as a remuneration for labor services rendered is absent in the Polish labor code. The direction of change is also telling. Thus, paragraph 13 has received a new non-economic meaning, imposing new, albeit unspecified, demands on employers, but at the same time the old paragraph 12, requiring due diligence from employees, has been eliminated. The code retains from the communist past even the so-called social functions of the firm requiring employers to satisfy 'social and cultural needs' of employees! All these and many other, more specific (and directly cost-increasing) provisions will affect the cost of labor for the employers. A major consequence is widely expected to be detrimental for the registered employment, pushing the private sector into the 'gray zone' rather than encouraging the shift in the opposite direction.

It should, then, be no surprise that the Polish labor market is characterized by rigid wages and high (registered) unemployment. Let us begin with the wage flexibility issue. It is a well-known tenet of classical economics that flexible wages are equilibrating demand for labor. This prescription dating from the time of Adam Smith has not lost, as we shall see, its validity in the contemporary world.

In economic theory wage inflexibility results mainly from strong labor unions coupled, according to some theorists, with union decentralization. It is stressed that inter-union competition reduces their interest in taking the consequences of wage demands for aggregate employment into account due to the fear of being outbid by a competing union. By contrast strong but centralized 'corporatist' unions allegedly better internalize the negative effects of rigid wages brought about by union bargaining power. However, recent literature, as stressed by Mickiewicz (1996), casts doubt on such differentiation pointing out that 'institutional sclerosis' in terms of Olson (1980) is the price paid by corporatist solutions and this, in turn, also reduces the positive effect of corporatist arrangements on wage flexibility.

Other institutional characteristics that contribute to wage inflexibility are those concerning the scheme of unemployment benefits. A high level and – even more – a long period of unemployment benefit payments, reduce the interest of the unemployed in the search for alternative employment. Liberal eligibility criteria work in the same direction; so do other determinants such as, for example, a wage tax. Altogether they reduce the risk associated with becoming unemployed, discourage early job search after falling into unemployment, and raise the reservation wage that entices an unemployed person to go back to work. Thus, all these factors increase wage inflexibility as the unemployed become less of a competition for those already in employment and do not exert downward pressure on wage level.

The foregoing institutional characteristics making for wage inflexibility are all present in Poland. Therefore, wages in Poland are inflexible downward in the face of high and very slowly declining unemployment (in spite of an economic boom). And yet wage flexibility matters for the level of unemployment. In Korea, for example, the crisis of the late 1970s (caused, incidentally, by a *dirigiste* shift in industrialization policy) resulted in the decline in real wages by 25 percent. The resultant reduction of labor costs positively influenced the level of employment and the speed of general economic recovery of the Korean economy.

In fact, we do not need to look to East Asian 'dragons' for a good example of wage flexibility and its impact on employment. The

Czech Republic (and earlier Czechoslovakia), a country with common communist history (but different *pre*-communist history!) is also characterized by a low level of unemployment. The Czechs are much more willing than Poles to trade real wage cuts for greater employment security. Also, Czech unemployment benefit eligibility criteria are much more restrictive than those of Poland. This also applies to the period of payment: in Poland it reaches 24 months compared with six months in the Czech Republic. These cases are very important for they show that traditional prescriptions of economics are as valid now, in post-communist countries, as they were in a pure *laissez-faire* economy like nineteenth-century England. If the labor market is not dominated by the unions and unemployment benefits do not strongly discourage the unemployed to search for work, then wages display flexibility, while unemployment is markedly lower than in countries with opposite institutional characteristics.

Another characteristic, wage and salary structure, is also affected by institutional features of the Polish labor market. The transition to a capitalist market economy had, as expected, a positive influence in this respect, the differentials increased markedly and typical distortions of a Soviet-type economy were corrected. As calculated by Rutkowski (1995), the wage ratio of those with higher education to those with elementary education increased from a meager 1.162 to a still relatively-low but nonetheless higher, 1.549 (data for 1994). Thus, returns to education, which is beginning again to be seen as an important part of human capital, have increased, as they should. However, given the influence of egalitarian pressures of trade unions in the state sector, these returns to education are lower in the state sector. The consequence is an outflow of the best skilled people from the state enterprise sector, because salary differences of those with higher education are the highest precisely in that educational category (26.1 percent in 1993). It should be signaled, however, that actual differences may be higher still, given the private sector's proclivity to often offer a part of the remuneration 'under the counter' so to say, in order to avoid paying the extremely high wage tax.

It is within the framework of interaction between registered employment, unregistered employment, unemployment and wage tax that it is worth looking more closely at the nature of high unemployment in Poland. We have already stressed the wage inflexibility in Poland and pointed to unions' aggressive wage policies and unemployment benefits discouraging job search, as major determinants. These wage policies differ from those known in the West. For in the West it is hardly possible to find SOEs that can afford a rise in wages and inevitably in prices of produced goods, then face falling demand – and still survive. In Poland it is possible, for they often do not pay their suppliers, banks, and even taxes and social security contributions.

There are, however, other factors at work. One is a large 'gray' or informal sector in the economy. It may be in part a legacy of the persistent excess demand for goods and services under communism and the flourishing supply of both at much higher, market-determined prices. The advent of normality changed, of course, the price relationship between registered and unregistered sale of goods and services. It is the untaxed, unregistered market that now offers goods and services at a lower price. The substantial increase in the size of the 'gray' market in terms of employment and GDP after 1989 has been determined by certain other factors. The first is another part of the communist legacy, that is demoralization. Low business ethics certainly contribute to the continuous existence and – in the early transition – also to an increase in the 'gray' sector as the opportunities for economic activities increased after 1989.

But the foremost factor throughout the post-1989 period has been an enormously high level of wage tax and associate payments (unemployment fund, etc.) amounting to almost 50 percent of gross wages. 'Gray' employment, covering both those employed without registration (and therefore without paying any taxes) and those receiving a part of their remuneration 'under the counter' (presumably an even larger number of people), is a response of the private sector to the high cost of an excessively – in fact: unreasonably – generous social security system.

These features of the Polish transition economy also contribute to both wage inflexibility and high registered unemployment. The unemployed, as stressed by Góra (1994), are not – as would be expected under more normal circumstances – a less expensive alternative to those presently employed. A combination of the long period of receiving benefits expected by the unemployed and their good prospects of an unregistered part-time or full-time job, reduces the need to search for work.

Phelps (1994) stresses that wage taxation, usually introduced to cover a variety of welfare state expenditures, is a very strong determinant of the rise in the natural rate of unemployment. Let us add that just as the rise in the taxation of factor labor in Western Europe has been higher than in the United States, helping to explain correspondingly higher unemployment rate in the former, so a high wage tax in Poland helps to explain the high unemployment rate here.

The monetarist prescription should be interpreted in accordance with the specific conditions of Polish transition. Thus, the unregistered employment of the unemployed in the 'gray' economy – estimated differently but often centering around the one million figure – puts actual unemployment rate in the last two to three years at the range of 8–10 percent rather than 14–16 percent. However, a downward adjustment of unemployment rate, allowing for the 'guesstimated' share of those actually working in the 'gray' economy, is definitely not the only adjustment to be made to take account of the specific conditions of Polish transition; the other side of the coin is hidden unemployment: excessive employment in the state enterprise sector. In industry, for example, approximately 55 percent of aggregate employment is still concentrated in state enterprises. And almost half of those firms are loss-makers, some of them beyond hope of a turnaround. A substantial part of the employment in mining, and a smaller but still-significant part of employment in other industries (steel-making and heavy engineering in the first place) have no economic rationale. In some cases the only economic solution is enterprise closure, in others it is slimming down. Altogether, a guesstimate that hidden unemployment is equal to between a quarter and one third of aggregate employment in state industry will not be far off the mark. In numerical terms it would amount to 500–660,000 employees.

To the foregoing one should also add hidden unemployment in private agriculture. Some official estimates by the Central Statistical Office (Witkowski 1995) put the figures of employment without any economic rationale between 150 and 330,000. But in family farming, adjustment takes place much more slowly, in line with opportunities for outside employment of family members. Thus, it does not need to be taken into account in an estimate of the size of actual upward adjustment of the registered rate of unemployment.

However, the actual unemployment rate of about 2.5 million people minus about 1 million of those employed in the 'gray' economy plus about 600,000 of those employed in the state sector without economic rationale plus a fraction of hidden unemployment on family farms yields a figure only somewhat lower – by some 300,000 – than actual unemployment. Translated into an unemployment rate it would amount to 12–13 percent. This 12–13 percent, we would assume, is the presumed natural rate of unemployment in the specific institutional conditions of the transition period in Poland. The Polish natural unemployment rate seems to be higher than in other countries undergoing successful transition. It is higher than in Hungary, given the much greater imbalance between labor and capital in Poland than in the latter country, while other institutional characteristics do not differ drastically between the two countries. And it is very much higher than in the Czech Republic, given both the different relationship between labor and capital in the latter country and much greater wage flexibility and less distortionary unemployment benefit scheme there. Interestingly, as Mickiewicz (1996) points out, estimates of the natural rate by Burda (1993) confirm the foregoing analysis. Burda's estimates yield for Poland a natural unemployment rate of 12.2 percent, which does not differ from the (much safer) range 12–13 percent suggested by this writer. Also, Poland, according to his estimates, has the highest natural unemployment rate in East-Central Europe.

The fact that the natural rate is high stems from the influence of determinants explained so far. They do not exhaust the list of institutional barriers to smooth functioning of the labor market. In a special paper prepared for this report (Góra et al. 1995), it is stressed that the system of unemployment benefits that makes school-leavers eligible to receive them is not only costly but also increases unemployment among the young. Unemployment benefits for the young undermine their motivation to search for jobs and, in the process, reduce the probability of their finding employment (as this probability decreases, on the average, with the time passed between leaving school and the time spent without a job). Their assessment of the system of unemployment benefits is on the whole very critical. They especially strongly criticize the already stressed long payment period of unemployment benefits already emphasized here. Empirical studies of the Polish labor market confirm the hypothesis that for those unemployed less than a year, the availability of benefits reduces the search intensity and, accordingly, the probability of finding a job. This probability has been proved higher in the case of those who did not receive (or ceased receiving) the benefits in question. (At the same time, from the social policy vantage point, the same system does not prevent those receiving unemployment benefits from falling below the poverty line.)

The foregoing considerations evaluated the labor market from the vantage point of institutional characteristics affecting the smooth operation of that market and found a lot of features that affect the market in a distortionary – in some cases a highly distortionary – manner. In the light of these considerations a series of recommendations may be formulated (in the order of decreasing importance):

1 As the gravest distortion is that of the dominant influence of labor over capital, remedial strategies are called for. There certainly should be legislative changes creating a better balance of rights and obligations of labor, e.g., by introducing at a minimum the right to a defensive lock-out. Other changes in the labor code are also needed to reduce the burden of private employers (state employers too, but they are under a much weaker cost pressure anyway). However, the labor market balance of power has been heavily biased in favor of labor and nothing makes the needed legislative changes probable in the foreseeable future.

Since no legislation will change the facts of life, that is a low level of organization of the private business sector, parties favoring a capitalist market economy should encourage the self-organization of employers. The emergence of sectoral and regional voluntary organizations should create a countervailing power to the 'big battalions' of organized labor in the state enterprise sector. However, this can be remedied only over time. But here, too, the actual developments seem to be moving in the opposite direction. The submitted legislation, bitterly but unsuccessfully opposed by business organizations and opposition parties, envisages the creation of a single employers' organization, compulsory for all employers (including state firms' managers as employers!) that will remain *de facto* under the tutelage of the state.

2 With the natural rate of unemployment adversely affected by a very high wage tax, the high taxation of factor labor should also be tackled as quickly as possible. This is, however, dependent first of all on the preceding reduction in general government expenditures. However, as the boom years did not bring any reduction in the share of the budget and other state expenditures (including those of the social security system) – it has stayed at the level of 50 percent of GDP since 1992–93 – the prospects for reduction in the forthcoming years of less buoyant business conditions than in the 1993–95 period are rather low until the 1997 elections and, maybe, beyond.

3 Extensive reform of the unemployment benefit scheme. The scheme needs substantial changes, first of all: (a) stricter eligibility criteria, with the exclusion of school-leavers from the scheme (they should be offered training and apprenticeships instead); and (b) reduction of the period of availability of unemployment benefits to a maximum of one year in well-specified circumstances. The level of benefits should be relatively high at the beginning, with graduated payments, decreasing as a share of the average wage, every three months.

The experience of Czechoslovakia and later, the Czech Republic, reveals that active labor market policies offering training for school- and university-leavers (the so-called assistant job program, in operation since 1991) are able to significantly reduce unemployment in a particularly vulnerable labor group. The main aim of the program has been to assist young people in their search for the first job through the supply of the working experience necessary for their future occupational or professional career (see, for example, Zamrazilova 1994). An imaginative program for secondary school-leavers (who suffer from the highest rate of unemployment, next to vocational school-leavers) is not beyond the capability of even a moderately competent government. As the proposed changes in the unemployment benefit scheme do not seem to particularly strongly and adversely affect any politically influential labor group, the political feasibility of the proposal is higher than that of any other proposal concerning the labor market.

4 The same applies to active labor market policies directly aimed at the reduction of unemployment. Here, an example of the Czech Republic points to measures reducing unemployment among school-leavers, especially secondary school-leavers. With respect to another group, that of the long-term unemployed, the problem is much more complex – and in Poland and other post-communist economies, also more difficult. The general observation points to the generally low level of skills of the long-term unemployed. Worse still, it is noted that their skills, already low, tend to decline further as a result of the loss of possibilities to learn on the job.

The more region-specific observation is that the group of low-skilled unemployed is in post-communist countries: (a) unusually large (mostly from industry); and (b) particularly resistant to any educational effort (or any other effort for that matter). The group is unusually large because one of the characteristics of the Soviet-type economy has been a disproportionally high demand for manual workers, unskilled and semi-skilled ones (Winiecki 1988). Also, given the erosion of work ethics (most clearly visible in large SOEs, from which most of the long-term low-skilled unemployed enter unemployment), they are particularly unwilling to upgrade their skills or learn new ones. This attitude is reinforced by the easy and long-lasting availability of unemployment benefits.

Therefore, recommendations here are not directed only at the group in question (as in the case of school-leavers) but also at the environment they operate in. Thus, recommendations to cut short the period of availability of unemployment benefits has already been formulated under item 3. Another recommendation concerns the reduction of severance costs for the employers. Since employment of low-skilled long-term unemployed carries with it the heightened risk of failure of the newly employed to adjust successfully to the requirements of the job, high costs of firing work against offering employment to the long-term unemployed. This risk would be reduced by the reduction of severance costs. Unfortunately, changes in the Polish labor code go in the opposite direction.

5 The next recommendation aims indirectly to reduce the natural rate of unemployment by reducing the size of the 'gray' economy. Clearly, the size of the 'gray' economy depends on the level of wage taxation. However, there is a roundabout strategy possible (in the sense of Hirschman (1963)) that would reduce the informal sector via a well designed carrot-and-stick mix. In particular, better legal protection resulting from the increasing consistency of business-related law and its application, as well as greater ability to use the services of the better-performing and increasingly sophisticated financial sector, would create strong incentives to register (either the firm or, more often, the true extent of its activity).

As rightly pointed out by Kornai (1992), any such program may easily err on the side of the stick, with little or no positive effects whatsoever. For the aim is not to suppress the unregistered sector but to entice employers to step out of the shade into the full daylight of registered activity. To achieve this, business people considering such a move should see advantages of that move outweighing disadvantages. Alas, given the communist heritage of the present ruling coalition, their inclination is to do the reverse of what is obviously necessary in this respect.

6 Various pieces of social security legislation (to be discussed in Chapter 6) should be coordinated with labor legislation so that by-products of the former do not affect adversely the latter. To exemplify the foregoing, it is recommended that the rules on early retirement should not allow (above a certain level) the parallel receipt of pension and income from employment. The recent Polish developments that enabled employees to combine a pension (often resulting from early retirement) with only a fraction less than full-time employment – often at the same job they held before receiving their pension – contributed indirectly to an increase in unemployment by reducing the availability of jobs. Moreover, this adverse effect has been compounded by the high cost of paying pensions earlier than would have been possible otherwise. For many early retirees would not have decided to retire earlier if they had not been offered such an opportunity to receive double income.

A brief look back at the institutional barriers concerning the labor market, recommendations for change and the political economy assessment of the feasibility of their implementation, suggests low probability of achieving the necessary changes, needed for the smooth functioning of the labor market. Thus, in all probability the most distortionary features of the Polish labor market will continue to exert their adverse influence for the foreseeable future. The room for positive change is undoubtedly limited.

There are two more recommendations to be made for the medium to long run. The first concerns Social Charter recommendations that may be pressed upon Polish authorities from two sides. On the one hand European Union authorities will press for the acceptance of a variety (of the otherwise non-compulsory) practices elaborated in the Social Charter in order to reduce the competitive edge of Polish producers resulting from the labor cost differential. On the other, Polish trade unions and political parties catering to the industrial labor electorate will try to achieve the level of benefits and protection under the banner of 'non-discrimination' of Polish workers. However, a rise in the already-too-high level of benefits and protection of Polish workers would be disastrous for the competitiveness of Polish industry. With productivity so much lower, with work ethics inherited from the communist past, and with greater imbalance between demand for and supply of saving and investment, Polish enterprises need any advantage they may possess in order to stay competitive.

In an even longer run another recommendation seems to be in order. Polish society is – to put it in plain words – poorly educated. Over two-thirds of the adult population has completed, at a maximum, a vocational school, elementary school or even less (low quality of vocational education makes things even worse). This legacy is thrust upon it at the time when systemic change puts human capital at a premium – and an increased premium at that. For the market economy of the future will require higher skills and an ability to continuously upgrade or change existing skills. Apart from the economic benefits of a better educated labor force, the expansion of education will bring also political benefits, including greater acceptance of changes taking place in Poland. There will be more about that in the final chapter.

5

COMPETITION AND OPENNESS UNDER GROWING INTERVENTIONIST PRESSURE

Jan Winiecki

In the process of transition from plan to market, competition and economic openness play the crucial role. The singular: 'role', rather than plural: 'roles', is proper here. The domestic price liberalization brings competition only to some areas of the national economy, given the monopolistic organizational structure of the Soviet-type economic (STE) regime. Elsewhere, competition has to be 'imported' through foreign exchange and foreign trade liberalization. Thus, apart from other, 'classical' benefits of external liberalization (specialization, importation of the 'proper', i.e. world market, price structure to the distorted STE regime), an extremely important benefit has been importation of competition.

This is exactly what happened in Poland. The unrestricted right of establishment in all sectors of the economy and in all areas of activity has given a strong impulse to an exceptionally dynamic expansion of the generic private enterprise sector in general and to the injection of competition even into a part of the state enterprise sector.

The interaction in this respect was best described by Gomułka (1992). He saw particularly beneficial consequences of the free entry of the private sector into both domestic wholesale trade and foreign trade. Private wholesalers were much quicker than old state-owned mammoths in identifying the products for which there was a large and unsatisfied demand and signaled these consumer preferences to producers. The faster identification of shifts in the structure of

55

demand created a (positive) stimulus for producers to change the structure of supply.

The other component of this interaction has been a threat. For external liberalization made it possible for domestic private wholesalers to import higher quality goods. Thus, domestic producers faced a threat of financial loss or even bankruptcy at the extreme as a price for non-adjustment to the changing structure of demand. These twofold adaptive pressures, positive (stimulus) and negative (threat), affected not only private producers but also some state-owned producers. In this way an injection of competition through the opening-up of the Polish economy facilitated structural adjustment in general and the shift of Polish exports westward in particular. Thus, openness allowed Polish (and not only Polish) economy to 'import' competition. It is worth noting that, in a truly Hayekian and 'supply-side' manner, the disciplining role of a threat may have been enough to force domestic monopolist, state-owned enterprises to adjust (even without actual imports to have taken place).

In reality, although there have been few bankruptcies (especially of state mammoths), industrial output fell heavily. This should have been expected (see Winiecki 1990b and 1991), although for reasons unrelated to import competition. Industrial output fell heavily at first, as the economy shed that part of demand that was the result of the wasteful nature of the old system. It is worth remembering that imports in fact fell in Poland in absolute terms in the first year of transition, while the largest fall in industrial output was registered precisely in 1990. In fact, as stated pointedly by Kornai (1993), output would have fallen anyway, even without a transition program comprising far-reaching external liberalization. Ukraine, an economy that left the wasteful Soviet economic system but landed nowhere near the minimum of a market system, is a case in point.

Industrial output recovered in the third year of transition and has been growing ever since at an elevated rate. However, whether in decline or in recovery, calls for greater protection from foreign competition and for other forms of support, under the name of industrial policy, have been insistent. They have also, since late 1991, been increasingly accommodated. Thus, in Poland a trade regime relatively close to free trade lasted about a year to a year and a half (Csaba 1994).

A question may be asked as to why the popularity of the slogan about 'the defense of the domestic market' (as well as demands for 'industrial policy') have had influence regardless of which coalition, liberal-conservative or ex-communist one, have been in power. The answer is relatively simple (and referred to already in Chapter 1). Both the Solidarity trade union and its political allies on the one hand, and ex-communists on the other, have their power base in the same segments of the economy: the state enterprise sector and the so-called 'budget' sector. Thus, resistance to calls for defense of a very large part of the former, unwilling or unable to adjust to the requirements of the market, has been weak in each case. The situation has been, however, more damaging under the rule of ex-communists because the only thing they learned in the past (in practice, not in textbooks on central planning, useless even then) was that economic policy-making means intervening on a case-by-case basis rather than through setting rules. Thus, Polish protectionism, apart from protection of agriculture, has been built in a haphazard, reactive way. As stressed already, the first wave of tariff increases started in late 1991 in response to various calls for protection. Then, in 1992, budget deficit pressures, combined with the said calls for protection of the Polish automotive industry, resulted in a dramatic rise in the level of protection, both tariff and non-tariff, of the industry in question. A very costly and consumer-unfriendly contract with Fiat to rescue the major Polish carmaker has been made a part and parcel of the whole protectionist set-up. The low regard of users for Polish automotive equipment, and the resultant increases in imports, brought about further protectionist measures with respect to vans and lorries. Soon, protection of the tractor industry followed suit; then, consumer electronics, and so on. The actually accorded degree of protection has been largely a function of the political influence of a given pressure group.

Growing protection has been inevitably intertwined with the demands for 'industrial policy'. The debate on the merits and demerits of the activist approach to branches and sectors of the economy continues throughout the post-World War II period. As stressed in a special paper prepared for this report (Wellisz 1996), the case of the superiority of an industrial policy approach rests, roughly speaking, on two assumptions. The first assumption is that bureaucrats' business acumen surpasses that of businessmen and they can identify business opportunities better. The second – and inseparable – assumption is that bureaucrats dispose more wisely other people's money than businessmen spend their own money. To say the least, both assumptions are implausible.

Since economics-based argumentation in favor of 'industrial policy' is pretty thin, they are often merged with more vaguely defined ones of the 'strategic' nature of some industries and/or their importance for maintaining economic sovereignty. The story has not been much different in Poland in this respect. The tendency of calling *any* industry strategic to obtain some kind of support, including respite from normal competition, has been very noticeable in the post-1989 period. Historical arguments have also been raised in the Polish debate. Protagonists of industrial policy insistently pointed to cases of what are popularly regarded as successful industrial policies, that is of Japan and the so-called East Asian 'dragons'. The interventionists' case is, however, rather weak, contrary to strongly-held beliefs.

To begin with, it is worth asking a simple question: why something that failed more or less conspicuously everywhere else (industrial policy, that is), has been a success in Japan. There are two answers, neither of them very comforting for protagonists of industrial policy. First, the Japanese are doing it better due to unique factors (specific culture, social structure, values, etc.) and, therefore, the success cannot be repeated outside the area where such unique factors dominate. It should be noted that other cases, those of East Asian 'dragons', remain within the same cultural area! Thus, if the success cannot be repeated outside that area, then industrial policy that failed everywhere outside that specific area is not worth trying.

Second, if it is not unique factors, then, given the poor record of industrial policies around the world, it is quite probable that other factors than industrial policies made these countries an economic success story. It is true that, except for Hong Kong, successful East Asian countries deviated from the free market doctrine. However, they deviated by much less than other countries around the world. It should be remembered that from the 1940s till the late 1970s the intellectual climate was definitely much more sympathetic to interventionism. Thus the Japanese, and later the South Koreans, Taiwanese and Singaporeans tended to follow the prevalent climate (a point made by Prowse 1993).

Fortunately for them they intervened less and therefore market forces played a much larger role there than in more dirigiste developing countries, to say nothing about the communist world. Thus, industrial policies in East Asia might have been more a hindrance than an advantage (and most probably they were!). The fact of being closer to the market rules of the game made them less damaging and, therefore, did not prevent these economies from succeeding, where more interventionist economies failed.

Of critical importance has been the export orientation of these economies. For in such economies any policy errors are revealed much faster than in inward-oriented economies, thanks to the warning signals from the world market, a point that was already being stressed in the professional literature by the early 1980s (see the special paper on participation in the world market and economic growth ('Uczestnictwo . . . ,' 1996)).

Apart from these general arguments against uncritical acceptance of what is offered as a historical case for industrial policy, there are specific arguments against it for the post-communist countries in transition. Thus, the policy of nurturing growth of some industries, even assuming that it may turn out to be a success (a less-than-plausible assumption!) cannot be repeated in economies whose main structural task of transition is to *reduce* the share of industry in the national economy rather than to increase it, as in developing countries. Besides, industrial policy, as it is usually sectoral in its applications, normally deals with either so-called 'advanced' or 'prospective' branches of the economy, or with 'problem' branches in need of adjustment assistance of one sort or another.

However, sector (industry, branch, etc.) based approach is particularly inappropriate in post-communist economies. One of the legacies of the past has been a very large variation of cost performance across state enterprises within the same branch. As enterprises were subsidized in the Soviet-type economic system, very bad performers coexisted for decades with relatively better ones. Thus, any industry- or branch-based program would inevitably waste money on trying to turn around hopeless cases.

A review of interventionist arguments, associated with Polish industrial policy-making, does not reveal any coherent pattern of thought. This is certainly impossible to find on important components such as selection of what is worth protecting and how. Moving from ideas to actual policy measures does not help much either. As noted already measures are defensive, oriented almost exclusively toward problem industries – and often even toward individual enterprises. Whatever protection within the industrial sector exists it concerns state enterprises, not private firms. This is in concordance with the political economy of transition. Private firms are subjected to the discipline of the market and it is state-owned units that shift the field of the battle: as they lose in the market, they try to win in the political field to survive. And given their political clout they usually succeed.

The pattern of support comprises the range of commissions and omissions that together make up a range of supportive measures. Among commissions, tariffs and non-tariff barriers (quotas and other barriers) figure prominently, albeit haphazardly, as policy measures. Although tariffs vary, overall the level of tariffs today is higher than at the time of the collapse of communism (however, tariffs played then a smaller role than they do today).

The years of the rule of ex-communists have witnessed the rapid expansion of the system of quotas, excise taxes, concessions, and on top of that temporary exemptions. Overall, these measures now affect about 4,000 product groups, almost 25 percent of Polish imports (see the publication *Wprost*, 1995, No. 27). They create not only a pattern of protection but also a pattern of corruption (see, *i.a.*, Winiecki 1996).

Even more haphazard is the pattern of domestic subsidies and other forms of support. For it comprises not only sins of commission such as subsidies (e.g. for coal mining), but also those of omission such as the acceptance of late payment or even non-payment of taxes and social security contributions by often semi-bankrupt but always politically powerful state mammoths. There is no doubt about the pernicious effects of such a pattern on the observance of the rules of competition (all the more so when the state seems to be accepting lawlessness as a norm).

Yet another form of support, mostly for the state enterprise sector, has been state guarantees of credits extended by banks, domestic or foreign, to enterprises. Here again, more often than not, it is political clout that determines the issuing of such a guarantee. A large number of the enterprises obtaining such guarantees are those in need of drastic restructuring coupled with substantial slimming down (steel mills, mining enterprises, etc.). Consequently credit guarantees become yet another measure petrifying the outdated output and employment structures inherited from the Soviet economic system. A very worrying sign is the very rapid growth of the aggregate value of state guarantees (on the pattern of support, see Koronowski 1994).

Domestic support is increasingly channeled through a variety of state agencies that are seen as a more 'modern' form of government intervention than outright subsidies. The already-quoted author (Bobińska 1994) has counted no less than ten governmental agencies that receive resources for sectoral, functional or regional intervention, usually according to vague, imprecise rules. Agencies more often than not support inveterate loss-makers or *de facto* bankrupt cases. Resources are allocated sometimes in the form of loans, more often – as in the case of the largest: the Agency for Industrial Development (ARP) – they are outright grants. The volume of financial assets at their disposal amounts in the aggregate, also on the basis of Bobińska (1994), to 20 bn zlotys, which is an equivalent of the own capital of three or four Polish large commercial banks. Their joint impact helps to undermine the market criteria that, by and large, have been applied to non-financial firms by the banking sector.

Another, more systematic way of supporting the state enterprise sector was the law on financial restructuring of 1993 which created a possibility, within a limited time span (until March 1996), of reducing the enterprise debts to the banking sector, suppliers, etc., on the basis of a settlement between an indebted enterprise and its creditors under the guidance of creditor banks. It opened a window of opportunity for those heavily-indebted state enterprises which, according to an assessment of creditor banks, offered a promise of successful turnaround.

It remains to be seen to what extent the breathing space offered by these disindebtment contracts (about 250 altogether) will be used to restructure and privatize successfully. For benefits are largely a matter for the future, while costs of such an operation have already been borne directly and will continue to be borne indirectly. Directly, because banks that made extensive write-offs had to be recapitalized from the state coffer. Indirectly, because the gate was opened and enterprises (managers, trade union leaders) may feel encouraged in their spendthrift ways and, having again priced themselves out of the market, may clamor for a new round of restructuring. Coal mining is an industry where the process of reindebtment has already taken place.

But coal mining is also a case of creating anti-competitive barriers through administrative centralization. The establishment of seven state holdings out of a much larger number of independent mines, unsurprisingly, created incentives for reallocation of resources from better mines to worse ones. It also created stronger trade union pressure for wage equalization across mines within a holding. A new round of centralization has already been proposed by ex-communists, namely the creation of a monopoly: 'Polish Coal'

('Polski Węgiel'). Consequences of such a measure are, again, predictable. There will be further reallocation of resources from better holdings to worse ones, and further wage pressures for wage equalization across holdings (upward equalization, of course ...). The first wave of strikes under such a slogan had already taken place even before the creation of a coal mining monopoly in February 1996.

Thus, efficiency will continue to decrease, while costs will continue to increase. A large number of Polish mines are unprofitable and since our costs are already at the level of world market prices there is not one chance in a hundred that the situation will ever improve. Thus, adjustment is inevitable. However, the steps taken so far lead in the opposite direction, namely the creation of a coal monopoly that will try to shift the cost of non-adjustment onto consumers. But higher fuel, and consequently, electricity costs will make Polish coal users more vulnerable to foreign competition both in world and domestic markets. For it is a well-known feature of a monopoly that higher cost at a certain stage of the production process due to a monopoly position increases cost at another stage – and reduces the competitive position of enterprises in downstream industries (see, *i.a.*, McKenzie 1985).

The comparison of, say, French and British experience in cutting their coal mining industries down to size, shows the superiority of a model where capacity reduction proceeds, in some relation at least, to the market-determined demand level. The political obstruction to almost any change allowed British mines to maintain output, and especially employment, much above the market-determined demand. Once, however, the level of subsidy exceeded the threshold of political acceptability under the changed political circumstances of the Thatcher years, the whole industry had to undergo a drastic process of capacity reduction. Thus, lack of change for a long time cumulates change in a short time-span, making adjustment more painful. Poland, with its aggressive unions and timid governments, whose power base is state enterprises, seems to be doomed to repeat in the future the more painful British experience.

The administrative centralization, or support for existing monopolies, is becoming widespread, again. It is a part of the heritage of the present coalition. For the experience of the so-called 'real socialism' tells ruling ex-communists that an economy is run not only on a case-by-case basis but also run from the center. Therefore, the less economic units exist, the better (because the economy is then, allegedly, easier to run). The ruling coalition instinctively welcomes all attempts to create trusts, holdings, etc. because they reduce the number of players to what is seen by economically illiterate ex-communist *apparatchiki* as more 'manageable' levels. Consequently, old monopolies such as telecommunications or electricity, are for all practical purposes maintained, while new ones are being created, such as 'Polish Oil' ('Nafta Polska'), allegedly for 'strategic' reasons. More and more segments of the economy are adversely affected by reduced competition. This is in contrast with what has been taking place in other East-Central European countries in transition. To confine ourselves to the oil industry, in 1995 Hungary began privatization of its national oil and gas monopoly, by initially offering a 25 percent stake to strategic investors. The Czech Republic, after lengthy negotiations, sold 49 percent of shares in the two largest petrochemical firms to AGIP, Conoco and Shell. There is no doubt that in these two countries domestic firms will be in much better shape when trade barriers go down, and they will feel the full force of competition of firms domiciled in the European Union.

An inconsistent, temporizing, defensive 'industrial policy' of the sort experienced in Poland is damaging economically, regardless of how politically expedient it is for the time being. First, as stressed already, it is undermining the competitiveness of enterprises in other industries and, thus, threatening the vitality of the whole economy. Sapping the energy of the dynamic segments of the economy will adversely affect aggregate performance and this, sooner or later, will turn at least a part of the electorate against the ruling coalition. Second, it is not going to ensure the survival of protected industries in their present size and shape anyway, if Poland joins the European Union, and the ruling coalition maintains that that is also its primary goal.

In accordance with articles of the membership treaty, the level of tariff protection in trade with EU member countries has begun to be reduced, down to zero in five years, by 20 percent a year. There are some possibilities for non-tariff protection to last longer but it is obvious that extended protection will be for well-defined exceptions (such as in the case of the personal automobiles industry) rather than the rule. Thus, the pressure of foreign competition will increase step by step but the process is relatively fast and the neglect of adjustment may become very costly for enterprises in the industries concerned. In the end, the easy financing of loss-makers (the 'soft' budget constraint of Kornai 1979 and 1986), surviving under the transition process and an efficiency-reducing centralization, will turn out to be a handicap rather than a helping hand, as thought by interventionists.

It is worth emphasizing that it is not only the economics of the present protectionism cum 'industrial policy' but its political economy that is harmful for the longer-term prospects for the Polish economy. This thesis is not in any way surprising as it has found empirical corroboration everywhere. Thus, protectionism and subsidization through a variety of measures are predictably reducing efficiency. Less competition produces less concern for tight cost control. Less concern for cost level translates into less efficient production – with the usual consequences. But both produce something else, namely entrenched redistributive coalitions (in the sense of Olson 1965 and 1980) that will fight tooth and nail to maintain the distorted pattern of production. Thus, the so-called 'defensive', protectionist and industrial policy measures generate adverse consequences not only under the interventionist regime now, but they also raise the cost of policy change in the future. In fact, the entrenchment of such redistributive coalitions may raise the current cost of interventionist policy even against the wishes and plans of intervention-prone decision-makers. For these coalitions may press for increasing or widening the level or extent of intervention above those regarded as desirable and, given their political clout, they may succeed in doing so. Coal mining and steel-making are cases in point.

So far we have been analyzing the *dirigiste* pressures on industry, both extractive and manufacturing, as well as on electricity and telecommunications utilities. However, Poland also has its share of protection and subsidization of agriculture – a share that has been increasing since the ascent of the present ruling coalition, with the peasant party (PSL) as a junior but nonetheless strong partner.

The economics and political economy of agricultural support are too well known to be analyzed here in any greater detail. There are, nonetheless, some special factors that make Polish agricultural support even more difficult than that elsewhere. First, Poland experiences a very disadvantageous ratio of the share of agriculture in GDP to the share in aggregate employment. This measure of the sector's relative productivity is 0.25, on a par with only a few developed and middle-developed countries with highly protected agriculture (e.g. Japan). The problems are compounded by the sheer size of the sector. The peasantry makes up about a third of the population and about 27 percent of aggregate employment (data for 1994), while contributing on the average only 6–7 percent of GDP. The average size of a farm in Poland is small (6.7 hectares in 1994) and has been increasing only very slowly over the last 15 years (by 1.2 percent annually). The percentage of holdings below 5 hectares is 54.5 percent (again, 1994 data). By contrast, the share of relatively large farms, those above 20 hectares, is barely 3.4 percent.

Since small-holders make up the overwhelmingly large part of the peasantry and peasantry amounts to over a quarter of aggregate employment, any European Union-style agricultural support program would have to be prohibitively costly. This is best exemplified by the contrast between two sets of figures. The level of protection in the European Union, measured by Producer Subsidy Equivalent (a share of farmers' aggregate income resulting from price support and subsidies) is on average 49 percent, while in Poland, 'only' 15–16 percent (in 1992–93). However, given the share of agriculture in aggregate population and employment, the ratio of total transfers as a share in GDP is in the European Union 2 percent, while in Poland it is already 3 percent. Besides, as is well known from the European Union and elsewhere, protection tends to maintain an inefficient output and employment structure rather than promote its transition to a more efficient one. What a haphazard system of high tariffs, quantitative controls, countervailing duties and various input subsidies and subsidized credits does in reality, is to marginally raise the income level of small farmers (sometimes at a cost not only to town dwellers but also to the more efficient, specialized, larger agricultural producers). As the size structure and productivity levels of Polish agriculture are particularly disadvantageous, incompatible with the dynamically growing economy and growing income levels outside agriculture, the resources of agricultural support are used to prop up the unsustainable size structure of Polish agriculture. Worse still, this is being done without any visible acceptance by the peasants of the unpleasant reality. And the reality is such that there is no place in a country of Poland's size for over two million minuscule farms! Thus, the resources are spent on supporting current consumption, not for improvement in rural infrastructure, expansion of trade, tourism, and other services that would create new jobs for the marginal farmers, enticing them to abandon agricultural production. Since such a perspective seems to be unacceptable for the majority of supporters of the ruling coalition member – the peasant party (PSL) – no effort has been made in this direction since the 1993 election.

The scale of sectors clamoring for protection and domestic support is relatively large in Poland, in comparison to developing countries and middle-developed Western economies. This is, however, a political economy problem. It indicates the strength of potential resistance to transition policies. In terms of economics it is by now reasonably well known what should be done in terms of what may be called industrial policy. It is worth underlining again and again that the area of conflict between market-oriented, outward-looking strategies and state-oriented, inward-looking strategies has been well researched and, over time, institutional and policy recommendations have been formulated.

From the early 1950s till the late 1970s the state-managed, inward-oriented industrial policy was dominant in the so-called developing world and intellectually respected but decreasingly applied in more mature Western market economies. It was the increasingly visible failure of that strategy (or strategies) in the developing countries and the Soviet-type economies that converted many to what has been for more than a quarter of a century a rather unpopular view. The change in the tide of opinion, and arguments underpinning the change, have been well described in the literature on economic development (for the purpose of this report the special paper 'Uczestnictwo . . .' (1996) outlines the contending views and recommendations resulting from the experience of the developing world).

Thus, it is reasonably well known what should be the sensible, supply-side-oriented industrial policy. To the extent that this policy is to be introduced in the definitely different environment of the post-communist economy in transition, with its distorted output and employment structure, with its dominance of the state sector, etc., it should be supplemented by specific competition-enhancing measures. Thus, there should be two sets of mutually supportive policies introduced in the Polish economy.

The first is the one generally recognized as the desirable supply-side industrial policy:

1 The removal of barriers to efficient resource allocation. This largely includes measures classified in this report under different headings, that is, improvements in the performance of the factor markets. Without greater mobility of labor and capital even state

intervention will be much more costly than it needs to be. Greater factor mobility means, however, also easier entry and, what is more to the point here, also easier exit. For it has been rightly stressed recently (see Walters and Hanke 1993), that in order to ensure the probability of success, an economic system should at the same time ensure the possibility of failure (meaning: exit). If for one reason or another, the possibility of failure is eliminated, the only result achieved is not the certainty of success but the certainty of failure. In an economy such as that of Poland, the sheer size of the sector clamoring for protection will absorb an exorbitantly large amount of production factors (especially capital) demanded in the growing sectors, thus ensuring long-term stagnation.

2 The reduction in the level of tariff protection and elimination of non-tariff barriers. The protection of the domestic market that weakens the pressure to stay competitive (in transition economy the pressure to adjust to the competitive economy conditions in the first place) is not supportive of the oft-stated aims of industrial policy to support modernization and increased competitiveness in Polish industry. Believers in the guiding hand of the state or its superior knowledge are mistaken not only because the growth-of-knowledge theory tells them that the dispersed knowledge of the market is far superior to that of bureaucracy (due to the inability to transmit inarticulate, or tacit, knowledge in any other way than through decisions taken by economic agents) but also due to the more mundane misunderstanding of the nature of competitive advantage. In contrast to bureaucratic logic, such competence cannot be achieved through a once-for-all effort behind the walls of protection. Technological and other competitive advantage is a result of the interaction of the firm with other world market players and continuous adjustment to stimuli transmitted by that market. In other words competitive advantage is the never-ending process (on this point, see Eliasson 1987).

Of course, in spite of high-sounding pronouncements, Polish protection, as stressed already, aims almost exclusively at slowing down the adjustment process. However, even with an aim like that, there are certain limits that should not be exceeded for fear of irreparably undermining the process that the policy is only attempting to slow down. Within such a perspective, it is worth inquiring whether the degree of protection imposed on the Polish economy is not already close to such a danger.

3 An introduction of a range of important, non-discriminatory supply-side measures may improve the performance of industry due to: (a) demonopolization and protection against unfair competition; (b) human capital enhancement; (c) support for basic science, dissemination of scientific and technical information, (d) incentives for attainment of international quality standards, (e) protection of intellectual property rights, etc. Here some progress has already been achieved but necessary changes in the tax laws, as well as well-designed budgetary support, are still a matter for the future. The weakest part is, of course, demonopolization, for it runs counter to the inherited philosophy (or, more realistically, Pavlovian instincts) of the former communist apparatchiks and bureaucrats now largely running the economy.

4 The introduction of minimal but enforceable environmental standards. Also necessary, although this time not non-discriminatory at the industry level (because of the obviously different environmental impact of different industries), is the policy enforcing standards of environmental protection. In a country where economic agents inherited from the communist past a blatant disregard for the rules of environmental protection, the strengthening of law enforcement is more important than the level of standards themselves. Standards should be gradually raised over time so as to ensure continuous environmental improvement. It should be remembered, however, that the big decrease in pollution is achieved in post-communist economies in transition, at the start of the process without any tightening of standards or even their enforcement, only due to the cut in output of the most environmentally damaging heavy industries. Therefore, gradual raising of standards should be correlated with the improvement of the competitive capacity of the economy. The strict enforcement of moderate standards is much better than introduction of unrealistically high and haphazardly enforced standards.

The foregoing, apart from item 4, has not been a particularly innovative formula for industrial (or more widely: sectoral) policy (in the Polish context see earlier proposals in *PPRG Report* (1993)). But there is not much that can sensibly be added, where general principles of non-discriminatory, supply-side policies are formulated. Whatever additions and/or modifications are proposed, they concern issues that are country-specific (and in some respects also region-specific).

Thus, the free entry and exit principle runs counter to the clamoring for support for many non-viable economic units. Therefore, on economic theory grounds, certain principles of temporary and selective support should be formulated and applied with respect to oversized heavy industries. The first principle should be the support for employees rather than firms. For it is at the level of the individual that the probability of adjustment is greater than at the level of the firm. However, even here the support should be well designed so as to avoid the outcomes such as that in coal mining, where extremely generous payments lasting two years have been instituted for those who were made redundant so that miners would use time and money to change their skills, become self-employed and/or move to their regions of origin. However, after two years, the miners, young and old alike, are back knocking on the doors of their old mines which continue to be severely overmanned anyway (Dziadul 1995).

At the enterprise level, any support should realistically be seen as based on political, not economic grounds. The already-mentioned principle of gradual adjustment should nonetheless be attempted through a clearly specified level and period of support as well as the rule establishing the sliding scale of decreasing support over time. Political economy of intervention tells us unambiguously that it is very difficult to withdraw support, once given, but future transition-oriented government should at least try to be firmer than the governments to-date (both non-communist and post-communist ones). Problems of support-through-slowing-down-adjustment would become considerably less important by accelerated privatization. Quite clearly, private enterprises behave differently. But here once more we come up against the stumbling block of Polish transition. In contrast with many other countries in the post-communist world, privatization in Poland meets strong resistance from different quarters. If and when such an attitude is going to change, remains to be seen.

In some heavy industries (mining, steel-making, bulk chemicals) the problem is overcapacity in the face of shrunken domestic and world markets. In others the problem is to create a structure that would move these industries toward the greater efficiency that would result from applying a well-designed mix of privatization cum competition and supervision. In those industries that are closer to what is often (wrongly) defined as a natural monopoly, such as electricity and heat generation and distribution, or telecommunications,

there are already reasonably well-designed institutional arrangements. The problem is, again, the resistance to privatization (as in
electricity generation) and the unwillingness of post-communist
governments to abandon discretionary policies (read: 'adhockery')
that bring in both political benefits and personal gains in favor of
a combination of market cum supervision, according to clearly
established rules (along UK or US lines), to say nothing about the
invisible hand of the market.

6

THE SOCIAL SECURITY SYSTEM

Prospects for changing the pension scheme

Aleksandra Wiktorow

Since 1989 a reform of the social security system has been subject-matter of various, often alarming, presentations, showing how high are the expenditures borne with respect to old-age and disability pensions, as well as how much money the budget spends in the form of subsidies to the social security system. Severe crisis of the system has been repeatedly predicted. Retirement (old-age) pensions and disability pensions, which entail about 80 percent of the expenses, are the largest component of the social security system.

The bad financial situation of the social security system in general, and of the pension scheme in particular, is largely the result of the problems inherited from the 1980s and those generated by the transformation itself. As in the case of the economic component of transformation, some mistakes – resulting in excessive increase in expenditures – were made in the social component as well. Some particularly wasteful decisions could have been avoided, whereas consequences of other decisions have often been difficult to foresee.

However, the conditions existing in the early transformation period (1989–90), when the estimates were made, should also be taken into account. It is worth remembering that, at the time, unemployment was expected to reach the level of 400,000 people only, and the arrangements proposed, as well as financial estimates, took such numbers as data. Unfortunately, not all predictions have proved to be correct and not all decisions taken in the social sphere turned out to be right, either.

Nonetheless it was only possible to introduce far-reaching

changes in the pension scheme in that early period. Later it proved to be politically impossible. From the perspective of the reform of the social security system, even the above-mentioned wastefulness may have its 'silver lining'. Presently, the necessity to, and inevitability of, reform to the system is clearer than in the past. Opponents of reform are willing to agree to moves much more radical than those which might have been accepted earlier. Even those who were against any changes involving limiting old-age and disabled pensioners' rights, perceive the need to reform the system. The costs of delay are enormous, and undoubtedly adversely affect economic growth. But they can be seen as the price that had to be paid for social acceptance of the reform and for the readiness of all political options to support it.

The pension scheme reform is often expected to result in an immediate and substantial decrease in expenditures. This can be evidenced by the statements to the effect that without launching an immediate reform, the scheme will go broke in two or three years. But any substantial reduction in expenditures resulting from reform can only be expected after a period of more than ten years. In the short run, they could be reduced in two ways: (i) through a decrease in the level of benefits (a renunciation of indexation would not be sufficient), or (ii) through a limitation of the number of old-age and disabled pensioners. Both solutions are politically impossible. At the end of 1995, the average value of an old-age and disability pension amounted to 490 zloty before taxes. It was almost 70 percent of the average wage and salary but less than $200. Thus, it is hard to say that the level of the pension is high, and that it can be decreased. Both old-age and disability pensions are granted for life. Only a part (38 percent) of disability pensions and family pensions (received, for example, by the children after their father's death, until they complete their education and by a non-working wife after her husband's death) are exceptions. In the first case a person entitled to a pension has to have periodical check-ups to determine if he or she can still draw a pension. In the second case, the right to draw a family pension for children ends after a child reaches a certain age. Proposals to lower the level of current benefits should be treated as purely theoretical.

With regard to the future, there is a possibility of limiting the number of new retirement and disability pensions by changing disablement rules, limiting the rights to early retirement and/or increasing the pension age. These changes will be achieved, however, very slowly and their effects will be felt with a long time-lag. The undoubtedly restrictive rules, adopted pursuant to the Pension Reform Act of 1991, are a good example. Their effects will be felt after a generational change in old-age and disability pensions.

One should acknowledge, then, that decreases in pension expenditures are not an immediate prospect and, thus, any future changes in the scheme should not aim at such short-term decrease. Furthermore, one should take into account the impact of changes in the pension scheme on the expenditures borne in other areas of the social security system such as social assistance or unemployment benefits. Similarly, changes in the organization and financing of the public health system may affect the revenues and expenditures of the pension scheme. Therefore, works on the reform of all areas of the social sphere must be coordinated. For example, financing family benefits from the budget instead of from the pension scheme does not mean that there are no such expenditures (and all the more so as the same institution deals, in large part, with the administration of those benefits).

In 1991 the liquidation of differences in the level of benefits granted in various periods to persons having the same job seniority and the same basis of assessment (i.e. the same salaries) was the problem of key importance. Other problems included elimination of non-insurance type elements of the scheme and its overall rationalization leading to increased effectiveness. Changes in the demographic structure of the population, which in the not-too-distant future could adversely affect the financial position of the state insurance sector, were considered as well. The main points of reform were:

- an extension of the period serving as the basis for calculating pension's level (basis of pension assessment) to 10 successive years chosen from the whole period of working activity (before the reform, the remunerations of the last 12 months only, were used for calculating a level of pension);
- a limitation of the periods for which the employee's unpaid insurance contribution did not affect benefits. There was a suggestion that the share of such periods was limited to a maximum of 25 percent of the whole working period, and to consider their contribution to the value of benefits at 50 percent of normal periods (i.e. the periods during which the employee's insurance contribution has been paid). Before the reform, the duration of

non-contributory periods was not limited and they had the same contribution to the value of benefits as the contributory periods;

- a limitation of the possibility of early retirement for various occupations and industrial branches, and the complete elimination of early retirement regardless of age. There was a suggestion that the level of pensions for each year of an early retirement should be reduced and that an increase in the employee's insurance contribution for groups entitled to an early retirement should be considered;

- an adoption of more stringent work disability criteria as a condition for receiving a disability pension;

- a strict limitation of the possibility to combine old-age or disability pension with actual employment, primarily in the case of individuals receiving early old-age pensions;

- changes in the principles of pension assessment. Given the impossibility of further rises in contributions and increases in the state budget's subsidies, a two-part benefits assessment was proposed. The first part was identical for everybody and equal to 24 percent of the average remuneration. Its purpose was redistributive. The second part was dependent on an employment period covered by insurance, amounting to 1.3 percent for each year of paid contributions and 0.7 percent for each non-contributory year;

- an elimination of so-called industrial branch allowances, which some groups of employees are entitled to. Altogether, over one million individuals, not including coal miners, were entitled to those allowances. These constituted over 18 percent of the total pension recipients.

- a limitation of the basis of assessment of old-age and disability pensions to the amount equal to 250 percent of the average wage or salary. It was necessary to limit the benefits' assessment to the suggested level in order to prevent manipulations of the basis of assessment in the last period before retirement;

- an indexation of the basis of assessment of all benefits granted before 1 January 1990 in order to restore parity between the bases of assessment for those retiring in different periods (with different rules of the game and different inflation levels).

The rearrangement of the basic pension scheme was to constitute the starting point for further reforms of the social security system. The rules, approved by the government in April 1991, were submitted to the Sejm in June 1991. Unfortunately, the Sejm adopted only a very abridged version of the submitted draft, containing only changes necessary to implement the indexation principles. The changes in disablement rules (not questioned by anybody), as well as limitations of early retirement due to the nature of work or the working conditions, were left unconsidered. The Senate introduced further amendments, taken into account by the Sejm, consisting of extremely beneficial rules concerning miners' pensions (both old-age and disability pensions).

When the Act was passed, it was first appealed against before the Constitutional Tribunal which recognized some of its provisions as incompatible with the Constitution. However, the Tribunal did not share the complainant's opinion regarding the unlawfulness of lowering the level of benefits granted before the passage of the Act. (See Trybunal Konstytucyjny 1991.) Before the Sejm's voting on changes resulting from the judgment by the Constitutional Tribunal, the government submitted other amendments, demanded, in turn, by the President, regarding indexation. The point concerned the right to combine the pension with employment for those individuals who had retired earlier due to a liquidation of their place of work (according to the Act adopted by the Sejm, a suspension of pension payments in the case of resumption of work before reaching the mandatory pension age was introduced). This was also questioned by the Tribunal. Finally, the Sejm decided that only the pensioners (old-age and disability ones) that had been receiving branch allowances before the passage of the Act would be compensated for those allowances (new pension recipients were not entitled to the branch allowances any more). Special certificates of participation (vouchers) in a mass privatization scheme were to constitute the compensation.

The actual effects of pension scheme reforms adopted in 1991 were as follows:

- a rise has been received by 66.7 percent of old-age and disabled pensioners, 19.3 percent of the benefits remained unchanged, and 14 percent have been decreased (these figures were changed further in favor of those who received increases);
- the bases of pension assessment have become more uniform and independent of the year of granting the pension;
- the number of low pensions decreased as a result of indexation, whereas the number of middle and higher ones increased. The so-called 'chimneys', i.e. high pensions resulting from artificially

increased wages and salaries in the last year before the retirement, have been liquidated.

Unfortunately, the Act of 1991 constituted the last stage of the reform so far. Further reform plans were not implemented. The only changes introduced concerned the limitation of indexation and were dictated by the necessity to decrease the level of subsidies to the pension scheme, as well as by the aim to make real growth in benefits no faster than that of remunerations. The changes, therefore, were not of systematic character.

The budget deficit was, however, growing fast, despite the fact that social security contributions were increased to 45 percent in 1992. An increase in unpaid contributions (primarily by big state enterprises), the existence of a 'gray' area of employment, and the high level of unemployment – all contributed to the growing deficit. However, proposals regarding further changes in the pension scheme encountered strong resistance from trade unions and the then opposition. Government activity concentrated on protecting what had already been achieved and preventing the return of costly and unworkable arrangements, which had been eliminated in 1991. Moreover, old-age and disability pension expenditures increased faster than was expected at the beginning of 1991 due to an enormous rise in the number of pensions. By virtue of earlier regulations, from the beginning of 1990 to the first quarter of 1995, about 620,000 employees retired early (in 1990–91 alone 400,000; in 1992 80,000; in 1993 62,000; in 1994 54,000; in the first quarter of 1995 24,000). Nothing could stem the tide afterwards. Once a pension right was granted it could not be taken away. Attempts to liquidate the early retirement pensions have met with a strong resistance, and the process of replacing them with so-called pre-pension benefits was a long one. They only entered into force in January 1995. Their impact, therefore, and the extent to which they will limit early pensions is uncertain as yet.

After the parliamentary elections of 1993, the new government promised to present, within six months, a draft reform of the social security system. Instead, several decisions impeding the reform have been taken. Since January 1994, minimum pension was increased by 4 points to 39 percent of the average remuneration. In particular, old-age and disabled pensioners who had been private farmers, have benefited from this rise. Analysis shows that 20 percent of minimum pensions are higher than the income formerly earned by those entitled to the pension in question. An increase in minimum old-age and disability pensions was an expensive mistake, which not only flattened the structure of benefits but also made it more difficult to make future necessary changes in the pension scheme (that it should go in the opposite direction, i.e. lower share of the redistributive part of the pension). Furthermore, an extension of some entitlements of coal miners working underground to brown-coal miners working on the ground has also been a mistake.

In May 1995, 'The draft program on social insurance reform. The provisions. The basic dilemmas. The questions' was submitted for social consultations. It was met with disapproval by theorists, practitioners in the field of social security, and the public opinion, primarily because it was introducing a relatively high state pension for everyone who retired at 65 years of age regardless of whether he/she had worked and paid insurance contributions before. Employee organizations have criticized the proposal to equalize women's and men's pension age at 65, since – in their opinion – it would result in an increase in unemployment among the youth. Moreover, the draft of the Ministry of Labor and Social Policy did not meet two fundamental assumptions of the reform: it was not reducing redistribution and it was not ensuring prospective decreases in expenditures. It did, in fact, just the opposite. In the first several years it would reverse the downward movement of current expenditures.

It should be stressed that construction of a new pension scheme is a relatively easy task. Quite helpful in this respect is the ongoing world-wide discussion on the future of base pension schemes, primarily in the light of the changing demographic conditions in the industrialized countries. The crisis of base pension schemes, and the necessity of overcoming it has arisen in many countries with different scales of intensity, irrespective of the existing model of pension benefits. Generally, everyone shares the opinion that the time of the single-pillar pension system is coming to an end (if it has not actually ended already). Everyone assumes a double- or triple-pillar scheme for the future. A multi-pillar system ensures greater income security both for the pension recipients and the state budget.

One of the most comprehensive analyses on this subject was presented by the World Bank (*Averting the Old-Age Crisis*, 1994) in its report on preventing a fiscal crisis resulting from the aging of industrial societies. I fully agree with the majority of opinions expressed by the authors of the report. Their purpose was to look for answers to the following questions:

1 Should the pension scheme be of a voluntary or compulsory character and at what level(s)?
2 What should be the relative importance of redistribution and individual contributions, and should they operate under the separate principles in one or in separate systems?
3 Who should bear the risk of unforeseen situations: the pensioners or the rest of society?
4 Should the scheme be based on financing from current contributions (pay-as-you-go principle) or capitalized ones?
5 Should the scheme be centralized or run by competing firms?

Every Polish author of a pension reform program should answer the above questions. The authors of the World Bank report are not in favor of releasing the state from all the responsibilities concerning problems faced by people of old age. According to them, entirely voluntary insurance schemes are insufficient due to the following reasons:

• the lack of farsightedness on the part of the employees and, consequently, the possible lack of any savings to make secure the old-age period and, in consequence, the necessity of supporting them by the rest of the society;
• the lack of relevant instruments to save due to poorly developed financial markets and the unstable economic situation observed in many countries;
• the incomplete insurance markets, adverse selection, and moral hazard which may result in the unavailability of insurance against some forms of risk for a part of society, for example the risk of inflation, of long life, investment risk, or the risk of economic crisis;
• an inequality of access to information. A part of society cannot and simply does not know how to assess the financial standing of private insurance companies and how to select the most suitable investment program. It is, thus, possible in such situations to make a wrong choice (from which it is difficult to back out later);
• the unavailability of private pension schemes for the poorer members of society who do not earn enough to make some savings for the future: Thus, redistribution which would prevent

poverty both during working life and retirement periods is needed. With regard to Poland, all the above statements are true.

The report comes to the conclusion that a single-pillar public pension scheme cannot fulfill all three functions at the same time, that is redistributive, insurance and savings functions. It is suggested that the savings function should be separated from the redistributive function and some other financial and administrative entities should be entrusted with the management of the two compulsory pillars of the pension scheme. The first redistributive pillar should be administered publicly and financed through taxes. The second should be administered privately and entirely based on capitalization. The third pillar, in the form of voluntary insurance programs for individuals who would like to receive higher income after retirement is also proposed.

The first pillar should be compulsory and at a modest level in order to ensure enough financial room for the remaining two pillars. It should be based on financing with current contributions. It should offer benefits either at a uniform level for everybody or make them partly dependent on income. This pension pillar should significantly limit the level of taxes (contributions) being paid in return for base old-age pension and, thus, limit the tendency towards excessive pension expenditures and unfavorable intra- and inter-generational transfers.

The second pillar should be compulsory, too, entirely based on capitalization of contributions, and privately administered. This should have a strong, positive impact on the increase in capital accumulation, development of financial markets, economic growth, and consequently facilitate financing of the first pillar of the adopted pension scheme. The second pillar could have a form of individual savings accounts or programs for occupational or professional groups.

The third pillar, like the second, could have a form of individual savings programs or the programs for occupational groups. It would be of an entirely voluntary character.

It needs to be emphasized that the role of the separate pillars will be changing according to the situation in a given country. However, each country should have a multi-pillar system. The report outlines a universal pension scheme model as an aim towards which all countries should strive, regardless of their stage of development.

The report also warns that one should approach the establishment of a multi-pillar pension scheme very carefully, taking into account the distinct conditions existing in each country, and the final model should not be expected to be achieved quickly. An introduction of voluntary and, next, compulsory programs, requires the following conditions to be met: a low rate of inflation should be achieved, direct control over interest and exchange rates should be eliminated, reliable savings institutions should be accessible to all citizens, a legal system that stimulates confidence in banks, insurance companies, and other financial institutions should exist, an efficient tax system should be in operation and, finally, human capital, necessary to effectively manage a financial system, should emerge.

No one can claim that Poland has already met all these conditions. Before this takes place, many questions concerning existing schemes, a comparison of them with schemes applied in other countries, and possible future arrangements in various walks of a socio-economic life – all need to be answered. The ways of implementing a triple-pillar system differ, depending on a country's level of development. The World Bank report distinguishes developing economies characterized by a low level of GNP per capita, maturing economies, and mature economies with an already extensive public pensions scheme (OECD, Central and East European countries, as well as the countries of Latin America have been included in the last group). In the case of this last group of countries it is suggested that the following steps be undertaken, while carrying a new system into effect:

- an increase in the retirement age, a decrease in the level of social benefits, a simplification of the structure of benefits, a reduction of the contribution rate and an extension of the base constituting the basis of contribution assessment;
- the creation of a second pillar should be achieved by a gradual reduction of the scope of the public pension scheme, with a simultaneous reallocation of contributions to the second, compulsory pillar; the maintenance of benefits at a relatively stable level (on the condition that it is low); and the transparency with regard to accumulated contributions within the framework of the old system should be accomplished (this requires the preparation of a politically and economically justified method of this transparency, as yet undetermined by the authors).

The foregoing proposals for the future have been presented to show that the process of seeking novel solutions to the pension problem by different countries finally leads to similar conclusions. The outline of changes laid out in Poland in 1991 were to follow the directions recommended by the World Bank. The future Polish pension scheme should be multi-pillar and the ways of financing pension expenditures should be varied. In the base pension scheme, the purpose of which is to protect against poverty, the redistributive method of financing (i.e. financing from current contributions or from taxes) should continue; however, this pillar must be constructed so as to minimize the necessity of budgetary subsidies. In the second pillar schemes (with the exception of industrial branch schemes with a stable, long-run participation) and in third pillar schemes, the capitalization method of financing should be applied. However, in the second pillar, the scope of state regulation and control should be larger, particularly if participation in it is to be compulsory. Each scheme should be administered separately.

The base pensions should be assessed according to the principle that the same contribution entitles one to the same benefit. It would be, therefore, a centralized system. By contrast, the supplementary pension schemes should be decentralized, as each of them would have its own rules of operation, adjusted to participants' preferences. They would be compulsory if, for example, the collective agreement in a given factory or industrial branch provided so. For the remaining employees they would have to be compulsory in any case.

The risk of unexpected situations under the base system should be divided between old-age pensioners and the rest of the society, but on the condition that it does not mean better treatment for old-age pensioners than for actually working employees. In principle, under the system of supplementary pensions, the risk would be borne by the participants of a particular system, and if this were to be impossible, a reinsurance fund should be put into operation. This is a brief answer to the five questions posed by the World Bank, regarding Poland's future pension scheme.

It does not seem that any radically different model could be suggested for the Polish conditions. But the debate should cover the specific concepts of separate pillars and methods of their implementation. One should also take into consideration the need to achieve minimally acceptable living conditions for old-age and disabled pensioners: for those who already receive the benefits, for those to whom the benefits will be granted during a transitional period, and for those who will benefit only from new solutions.

Furthermore, demographic changes, as well as present and future financial constraints, should be considered. It should be kept in mind that the financing of the transitional period requires increased subsidies.

The changes in the pension scheme should be two-pronged ones. They should entail, on the one hand, the transformation of the base pensions' schemes, and on the other, the establishment of a system of supplementary pensions. As previously mentioned, the supplementary pensions will replace in part the pensions of the base system, which means that the shape of the base system will have a bigger influence on their (i.e. the supplementary pensions') development than the factors inherent in a supplementary system itself.

Regardless of the new final model of the pension scheme that will eventually be adopted, the costs of transition will be high. In each case the same problem emerges: that of finding the financial means to cover a decrease in receipts caused by the limitation of the level of contributions under a given selected base system. No one doubts any longer that the high costs connected with the transition to a new scheme will have to be covered by the central government budget in a direct or indirect form. Nowadays, nearly everyone points to mass privatization as a source of financing the cost of a pension scheme's transformation, suggesting different uses of means thus obtained, while usually overestimating the level of revenues from privatization and their importance in financing any pension's reform. It seems that there are the following possibilities of utilizing revenues from privatization in the reform of the pension scheme. First, the proceeds from the sale of privatized enterprises can be earmarked for a reduction of public debt. It would, then, be easier for the budget to accommodate new expenditures, resulting from the costs of financing the transition to a new pension scheme. This is a rational proposal. However, there is a danger that the money thus obtained will be used for other purposes, since in each year there is going to be 'a contest of aims'. Besides, such a way of using funds obtained from the privatization is not appealing from the political economy point of view since it is difficult to present to the public in an attractive way.

Second, a special fund earmarked for supplementary financing of the present and the future base pension scheme could be established. The purpose of this fund would be to relieve the budget of a part of subsidies and to cover the costs of transition to the new system. There is a good justification from a social standpoint that the elderly would also benefit from privatization in this case since the revenues derived from the capital created by them will be earmarked for old-age and disability pensions. So far it is primarily employees who have benefited from privatization. The old-age and disabled pensioners do not want to be perceived as a burden to the budget only. Thanks to the privatization-financed fund they would be less dependent on the budget. In the future it will be possible to lower the compulsory social insurance premium (old-age and disability insurance, as well as health and unemployment insurance being planned in the nearest future) thanks to the permanent revenues from such a special fund.

Third, the revenues from privatization can be earmarked to establish the financial foundations of pension funds for the present employees (some suggest that individual accounts be supplemented depending on their holder's age and job seniority). If such rules were adopted, the elderly people would feel wronged since they would be reminded of the fact that old-age and disability pensions continue to require subsidies. Furthermore, people currently working would obtain yet another access to the privatization 'pie'. The elderly people feel that the national property being privatized at present was created by them in the first place. Therefore, from the political economy point of view, it is far better to support the creation of new pension funds, financed only by participants' contributions (encouraged by tax exemptions) and by external capital.

Utilizing privatization assets for the purpose of supplementary financing of the public pension scheme during the transitional period is not very attractive from the political economy point of view. However it is less costly than financing the transition period directly from the budget and simultaneously channeling the proceeds from property being privatized to the private pension funds. For nobody knows whether economic growth resulting from faster development of private pension funds would be able to contribute to equilibrating the budget, given the expenditures borne to cover the costs of the transformation of the base pensions scheme. It is true, then, that the private pension funds, being established primarily from the participants' contributions, would develop at a slower pace, but the base pension scheme would be stronger.

It is worth remembering that in 1994, 261 billion old zlotys (equal to 37.9 percent of the state budget for the year) were spent on old-age and disability pensions (i.e. pensions financed from contributions). (*Note*: 1995 monetary reform slashed four zeros from the zloty; therefore 1 new zloty is worth 10,000 old zlotys.) This sum was bigger than the sum raised from public insurance contributions (from which the expenditures on other benefits have to be financed as well). Within the coming years one will have to finance the benefits for the present, relatively young, pensioners. The annual subsidies to the public insurance system amount to some 60 billion old zlotys, not including the expenditures on pensions for the individual farmers, as well as the army, police, and prison staff. All these expenditures should be kept in mind when drafting the new pension scheme.

The estimates of the value of assets that are to be privatized vary and even the most optimistic ones are quite modest *vis-à-vis* the needs of the transition budget of the pension scheme. Besides there are quite a few competing uses envisaged for the revenues from privatization. These are, apart from financing of pension scheme reform, also reprivatization; compensation for public sector employees (education, health, administration) and for pensioners as a result of the relevant decision of the Constitutional Tribunal; the financial restructuring of important industrial branches undergoing the process of privatization, etc. Thus, it is not clear how large a share of assets will be left for pension reform. The most advantageous would be if the value of the privatized assets was high enough to enable the annual revenues from these assets to cover as much as possible of the gap between annual revenues and expenditures on the transition period. These revenues, moreover, have to be at a rather stable level in the long run.

Having all this in mind, it is time to recommend the outline of a pension system for Poland. We begin by presenting the base pension system. Thus, each working person who receives an income to the value of at least a half of the minimum wage and who pays contributions to the pension scheme based on this income, would be subject to the compulsory pension insurance. At the other end of income scale, a maximum income subject to the insurance in question should be set as well, while taking into account the possibilities of the state financing the gap which will exist for a long time after the introduction of such a ceiling which at present does not exist.

It is not necessary to set such a limit once and for all, constituting, for example, a fixed percentage of an average salary. The establishment of three such limits for different groups of future pensioners would minimize future expenditures as well as give more room for the development of the supplementary insurance programs. We suggest a ceiling on the part of income that will be subject to contribution assessment and, accordingly, of base pension assessment (old-age and disability pension) of 250 percent of an average salary for those who are going to retire in fewer than 15–30 years, 200 percent of an average salary for those who are going to retire later, and 150 percent for those who have only recently started working. This would automatically ensure that the future base pension will be over time lower (but increasingly supplemented by pensions from the other two pillars of the reformed pension scheme).

Taking 1994 as a reference point, around 2.1 percent of the working population was earning above 250 percent of an average remuneration, 4.7 percent – above 200 percent, and 15.3 percent – above 150 percent. In 1995, with the hypothetical introduction of a reformed scheme, the loss of revenue by the state insurance system due to uncollected contributions from income above 250 percent of an average salary would increase the deficit only by around 900 million old zlotys. Due to a lack of data on the wage structure according to age it is difficult to estimate the results of the introduction of the three suggested income limits. Nevertheless, one may expect that the decrease in revenues would not be much higher, since the Central Statistical Bureau (GUS) data show that remuneration increases with a person's age. For example, if we assume that the average remuneration of an examined group of 9,266 persons (in May 1995) equaled 100 percent, then the employees at the age of 15–19 were earning 70 percent of the average, those at the age of 25–29 – 92 percent, 45–54 – 106 percent, and 60–64 – 127.7 percent. In the younger employees' group there may be a bigger differentiation of salaries and there are undoubtedly certain groups who earn a lot. It would not, however, significantly affect aggregate revenues from contributions. The introduction of lower income limits for younger groups will influence, to a greater extent, the financing of a reformed pension scheme in the time span of ten to twenty years. Then, the main contributing age group would become that whose income limit was set at the level of 200 percent. Later still, the main contributing age group would be that whose limit was set at 150 percent. An adoption of such a solution would extend the period of subsidization of the state insurance system (the first pillar), but on the other hand it would significantly decrease the scale of state support for base pension payment.

The decrease in revenues of the state insurance system caused by an introduction of a ceiling (or ceilings) on level of income subject to contribution assessment is probably the only unavoidable negative effect of the intended reform from the vantage point of public finance.

The termination of a labor contract after arriving at the pension age will constitute the basic condition entitling someone to a pension. Women's and men's pension age should be gradually equalized at the same level of 65 years. If women's pension age were increased by four months per year, then the equalization would occur after 15 years. The possibility to retire with pension at the age of 55 after working for 30 years would be eliminated. Only those women whose job seniority already amounted to 30 years at the moment the reform comes into force retain the right to an early retirement. Both women and men would be allowed an early retirement – up to five years earlier – on condition that the level of benefits they receive will be lower. An employee may work even after arriving at the pension age and then his pension will be increased for each year of the postponement.

An extension of women's retirement age would cause a reduction in the aggregate pension scheme's expenditures. Also, the fact that the person continues to be employed would result in their paying contributions to the pension scheme longer, while a pension granted later would be drawn for a shorter period. The pension would be higher but the excess pension would cost less than a pension, however lower, paid for up to five additional years. Despite an increase in the retirement age, women would continue to be privileged. For the same contributions they would still be receiving the benefits for a longer time due to women's substantially longer life expectancy after the age of 65 years.

The pension's level would depend on two elements: a social pension part (being of a redistributive character) and an insurance-based pension part, dependent on the basis of assessment, i.e. level of contribution-covered income, and the period during which contributions were paid. The proportions of those two parts would change in comparison with the presently existing scheme. The social (redistributive) part should be decreased by up to 15 percent of a base amount, while an insurance-based part should remain at the level of 1.3 percent for each year of insurance paid. This would substantially diminish the scale of redistribution in comparison with the present pension scheme. Persons that retired before the pension reform act came into force would keep their right to the hitherto existing benefits. Persons that are to retire in 10 to 15 years from now would have their pensions calculated on the basis of the old rules. Those younger would be granted composite benefits in proportion to the periods covered by the old and new rules. It is suggested that the basis of pension assessment be calculated on the basis of salary or wage of 20 years from the whole period of working activity (instead of 10 successive years as it is now, since 1991), or even the salary or wage from the whole period of working activity. This would be possible, of course, only after individual records of insurance contributions are introduced.

After the retirement age is increased, the problem of combining a pension with work will become less important. As for the present, the following rules should be applied. Recipients of early pensions could work only if the pension payments are suspended. Others could not earn more than the difference between the level of their pension and the basis of assessment. The pension is supposed to replace the lost revenue from work rather than be an addition to a salary or wage.

Indexation is, in the system of base pensions, the only flexible element which in the short run can affect the level of aggregate expenditures. Therefore, it should not be provided automatically by law, without the possibility of suspension or limitation of indexation, when financial difficulties arise (e.g. due to severe recession or other developments adversely affecting economic growth).

The entitlements to early retirement for those employed in particularly strenuous work conditions or in particular occupations are the most difficult problem to solve, apart from financing the transition to a new scheme. An abnormally large part of the working population is entitled to early retirement. Unfortunately, it is impossible even to determine the exact number since there is no statistical basis for such reporting. Approximately 20 percent of all employed may exercise the right to early retirement on the basis of so-called 'branch agreements'. Undoubtedly, those already entitled to early retirement will retain their rights under the new pension scheme as well. The issue of whether those who are not yet entitled, but are covered by the agreements in question should have their rights confirmed as well, requires a decision to be taken at the political level.

A specific solution needs to be adopted with regard to the mining industry, where a pension can be granted irrespective of the retirement age after working for 25 years underground. About 300,000 persons are currently employed in the mining industry and 250,000 old-age and disability pensions are being paid (out of which 124,000 are old-age pensions). It is planned that about 70,000 persons will be made redundant in the mining industry in the foreseeable future. Even if contributions were doubled in that industry, they would not match the expenditures on miners' benefits. Thus, the cost of reforming the miners' pension scheme has to be financed from the outside and treated as a part of the restructuring costs of the mining industry.

One may consider yet another solution: the introduction of transitional retirement pensions financed from branch-level or enterprise-level pension funds during the period between early retirement and the statutory retirement age.

In contrast to rationalization of the base pension scheme, which is relatively easy to recommend, the creation of the second pillar of the pension scheme, i.e. supplementary pensions, is much more difficult. The requirements in this respect have already been spelled out, as well as the assessment that Poland has not yet met all of them. This does not mean, however, that the process should not begin, at least in the sphere of regulation.

It seems that in Polish conditions those additional pension schemes that will be established at the enterprise, branch or occupational level, show the greatest probability of developing quickly. The employers, primarily large ones, have the opportunity to establish a pension fund for their employees. Even more favorable would be the conditions, already pointed out, where such a fund is established during privatization. Shares received by the employees could constitute the financial beginning of a supplementary pension scheme. Having the prospect ahead of a higher aggregate pension after retirement, employees might not sell their shares as has so often occurred in the last few years.

The systems of supplementary pensions should be voluntary. The incentives nonetheless should exist: first of all tax exemptions, to encourage the development of such schemes. Besides the above pension schemes one should expect the emergence of open pension funds accessible to everyone that would be subject to the same regulations. An alternative arrangement assumes that only those additional pension schemes which correspond to employees' lost privileges (see above) could be managed at the enterprise or branch level. The remaining private pension funds would operate on a free choice basis.

However, irrespective of the organizational form and the type of pension fund, certain issues must be regulated for all private pension schemes in a uniform manner. They are the following ones:

- participation in the scheme (minimum age, type of employment);
- entitlement to retirement pension (required period of contribution payments, waiting period);
- spouse's entitlement to pension after participant's death;
- portability;
- reinsurance of pension schemes, necessary to avoid fund insolvency (for example, due to employer's bankruptcy);
- requirements concerning trustees;
- supervision and control (with regard to membership rights, contributions and taxes, asset management, and reinsurance).

Certain limitations on the investment policies of funds must be made as well. According to some Polish experts, investment of the resources of an enterprise pension fund in one's own company should be forbidden or strongly circumscribed. Since the liabilities of the funds are of a long-term nature, the assets also need to be invested in long-term securities. These are shares (being the securities with no redemption date stated), and government and corporate bonds. There have not been long-term government or corporate bonds issued in Poland so far. Obviously, the effective management of assets is possible in a relatively well-developed capital market which ensures a steady supply of the securities of the required characteristics regarding risk and maturity and within the strictly defined legal framework, protecting the rights of pension funds' participants.

As one can see, the establishment of a strong, large-scale supplementary old-age pension scheme is not possible in the short run. The system of basic old-age pensions has to change first. Regulations in many areas are also needed. The fundamental issue is to exempt supplementary insurance contributions from income taxes (up to a defined limit expressed in money terms), since as the experience of many countries shows, this is the greatest stimulus to the creation of supplementary schemes.

Pension schemes for farmers, as well as for the army, police, and other uniformed services have not been addressed to any greater extent. This does not mean, however, that those schemes should remain unchanged. On the contrary, their change must be adjusted to the changes in the basic scheme for employees. Thus, some recommendations can be formulated as well.

The problem of individual farmers' pensions requires a different approach. Of course, farmers will strongly resist any additional financial burden for nobody abandons easily a privileged position. The fact that farmers cover only about 6 percent of their own old-age and disability pensions' expenditures should be recognized as such a privilege. The entitlement to a minimum social component of a base pension should be kept only by those farmers who own small, low-income farms or those who work on a self-sufficiency basis (do not sell produce on the market) – and even on the proviso that such entitlement cannot be given to more than two insured persons in a family. The remaining farmers should be treated as all other persons pursuing economic activity, and, thus, should pay contributions sufficient to cover the minimum pension benefits. In this case, the principles of indexation should be based exclusively on price increases. Such changes are necessary considering also the necessity of transforming the Polish countryside. The retirement or disability pensions cannot and should not constitute the main source of income for multi-generational farms, as is the case now.

Next, even if one assumes that expenditures on pension benefits for uniformed services have to be borne directly by the state budget, and that the principles of granting the benefits and the value of these benefits should be more favorable than those for the employees, the equality of treatment of all pensioners should be strictly observed, regardless of the system under which the old-age and disability pension are granted. Therefore, for example, the principles of indexation of benefits should be the same. There are no grounds for having relatively young army and police pensioners, whose benefits are, on the average, twice as high as those of employees' benefits, and who have the opportunity to work and earn more than allowed by the general rules. Also, the present calculation of the basis of assessment of a pension in the uniformed services needs to be reconsidered. At present, the salary from the last month of service, i.e. the highest received in the entire period of service, is taken into account when calculating a pension. It would be unfair to keep the existing principles for the uniformed services, while extending the assessment period for everybody else.

The financial situation of the state insurance is beginning to stabilize and it may even improve slightly in the near future. The positive effects of the 1991 reform are increasingly felt. The number of persons retiring will be small for several years. Unemployment is decreasing slowly and at the same time large numbers of young people are going to enter the labor force. All this will influence the contributions/expenditures ratio. The collection mechanism is going to improve, owing to new regulations. Thus, the next few years should be seen as the best period for launching the reform of the base pension scheme (and establishing the supplementary schemes). It is, therefore, necessary to take advantage of this 'breathing space'. If this favorable period is not taken advantage of, then in 10 to 12 years we will most probably face serious difficulties because of demographic changes in Polish society.

7

PROPERTY RIGHTS, PRIVATE SECTOR AND PUBLIC ATTITUDES TOWARD INSTITUTIONAL CHANGE

Jacek Szymanderski and Jan Winiecki

On economic theory grounds, especially neo-institutional economic theory grounds, there has never been any doubt as to the crucial role of the private sector – in fact: of the dominance of the private sector – for the market economy. Nor have there been any doubts harbored about the need for well-designed and secure property rights. On these points, see, for example, Pejovich (1990). Nor were there any doubts on historical grounds. No society ever succeeded in building a capitalist market economy (and there has never been anything other than a capitalist market economy) without the dominant private sector. To use an expression of this author, there is no capitalism without capitalists (Winiecki 1990a).

However obvious, these conclusions were clear only for a minority of the systemic change-oriented elite that came to power in 1989. The government program of October 1989, very specific on the need for stabilization and liberalization, stressed also, on the institutional side, the need for making the Polish economy similar to that of Western economies in institutional respects as well. Quite obviously for the minority in question, it also entailed privatization and, consequently, bringing the share of the private sector in GDP and employment up to Western levels (a 70–80 percent share at a minimum).

The privatization consequences were not, however, as clearly spelled out as were other parts of the program. Even the institution that was designed to accomplish the change was euphemistically called the Office (later: Ministry) of Ownership Transformation, without clearly spelling out what kind of ownership changes it was to accomplish.

There were reasons for this circumspection. A large part of the victorious political 'Solidarity' camp was for quite some time attracted by the self-management idea, in spite of the decisive theoretical criticism of self-management and the disastrous historical experience of the former Yugoslavia. In 1989 they still saw in self-management their beloved 'Third Way' to the future (and even succeeded in writing their belief into the 'Round Table' recommendations!). Apart from this specifically Polish problem, there were other more general grounds on which to expect the support for systemic change involving large-scale privatization to be rather shallow. After all, the generally criticized features of the state-owned enterprises (SOEs) were at the same time sources of additional material and non-material benefits for those who worked there. Thus, privatization, based on rightly assumed greater efficiency of privately-owned enterprises, would undoubtedly bring higher wages and salaries in the future but in the present would eliminate redundant labor, increase work discipline, reveal the incompetence of many, scrap the welfarism at the enterprise level, and markedly reduce theft and corruption.

Although it was perceived that there existed a general support for systemic change which promised to make the Polish economy more like any Western economy, it was rather obvious that the general support would not translate automatically into case-by-case support if and when a given enterprise was to be privatized. In this manner, the general reasons for resistance to change mix with the specifically Polish reasons. The probability of success of this resistance has been made stronger in Poland by the tradition of workers' militancy (since 1980 under the banner of 'Solidarity').

In the end, not only parties of the communist *ancien régime* and the utopian left wing of 'Solidarity' but also of the nationalist and fundamentalist-Catholic Right turned out to be hostile to privatization. Given such an unholy alliance, privatization proceeded very slowly. At that time such an outcome was regarded as a disaster. It is hardly surprising, though. At the very beginning of the transition process politicians, trade union activists, analysts and the general public concentrated their attention almost exclusively on the state enterprise sector. After all, the state sector dwarfed the private sector outside agriculture, and many sensible people tied their hopes for radical change for the better onto the transformation of SOEs into privately-owned ones (those less sensible did so onto the transformation of SOEs into self-management units). However, the much-resisted Polish privatization did not live up to those expectations. The contribution of privatization to the creation of the dominant private sector has been very small. Concerning the number of privatized enterprises, Bobińska (1994) calculated totals that sharply differed from official ones. To quote from her paper:

> Out of a total of 8,441 state-owned enterprises in 1990, 1,595 (18.9 percent) have been transferred to the State Treasury Agricultural Ownership Agency, i.e. a state-owned institution. 263 enterprises (3.1 percent) were communalized, i.e. taken over by local governments and 2,521 (29.9 percent) were transformed based on the above-mentioned law [of July 1990 – J.W.]. The remaining enterprises have not undergone any transformation.
>
> (Bobińska 1994: 34–5)

Bobińska also calculated that among those enterprises which are officially described as 'having undergone transformation' only 98 (1.2 percent) have been transformed into joint-stock companies and have had at least 50 percent of their stock sold, i.e have actually been privatized; 424 (5 percent) have been transformed but not privatized; 707 (8.4 percent) have been liquidated under the terms of Article 37 of the privatization law of 1990, including 85 enterprises (1 percent) that have been sold. In most of the enterprises, the assets are merely leased and therefore true privatization will have occurred only when they have been paid for in over 50 percent; a further 172 enterprises (2 percent) have also been liquidated according to Article 19 of the old law on state-owned enterprises; and there are 1,220 enterprises (14.5 percent) undergoing transformation. At the same time, 4,062 enterprises or nearly half of the total (48.2 percent to be exact), have not undergone any sort of transformation.

Bobińska (1994: 35) concluded that 'over the past four years privatization has been carried out fully and completely in only 1.7 percent of the enterprises according to the terms of the privatization law' of 1990. One may ask, however, whether the indicator used is not a misleading one, considering the fact that in a Soviet-type economy, most state-owned enterprises are large and very large, and consequently 1.7 percent may account for a much higher share of employment and production.

Helpful in this respect is a paper on the change in the ownership structure of the Polish economy prepared specially for this report (Chmiel and Pawłowska 1996). A very detailed analysis shows that the share of privatized SOEs in aggregate output and employment varies between imperceptible and small. In industry and construction, that is two out of the four branches of the economy examined in detail in the paper, shares in output at the end of 1994 stood, respectively, at 4.4 percent and 12.4 percent (somewhat less in employment: 4.1 percent and 11.3 percent). And those were branches with the highest contribution of privatized SOEs to aggregate output and employment. In the other two branches, trade and transportation, privatization 'from above' contributed in less than 1 percent.

Nonetheless, in spite of the failures of privatization, the share of the private sector in GDP simultaneously exceeded 50 percent of the total, while that of employment exceeded 60 percent – and since then shares of the private sector have increased again, given the disparity in output growth rates. Thus, in the aggregate, Poland does not differ much from other success stories of transition. This has been the case because privatization does not consist only of transformation of SOEs into privately-owned enterprises, but also the establishment of new private enterprises and expansion of the existing ones. Using the terminology applied elsewhere (see Gruszecki and Winiecki 1991) we may distinguish the privatization 'from above', that is the one attracting most attention, and privatization 'from below', the growth of the generic private sector from the ground up. Both ways contribute to the creation of an economy with an ownership structure similar to that of Western countries.

In Poland privatization 'from below' has more than made up for the weakness of privatization 'from above'. The Polish generic private sector outside agriculture produces almost 45 percent of GDP with over 35 percent of aggregate employment. And these shares have increased 3–4 times since the beginning of transition.

The reasons for the particularly dynamic expansion of the generic private sector, even in comparison with other success stories of transition, lie, first of all, in a more decisive policy of liberalization and deregulation compared with other countries of the region. Poland has gone farther than nearly all other countries in creating conditions allowing private companies almost unrestricted access to all sectors of the economy and areas of activity (such as, for example, foreign trade).

To begin with, the comparison of the unrestricted right of establishment in Poland with the various territorial, sectoral, and other limitations which still exist in other countries, makes it easier to understand the causes for the exceptionally dynamic growth of the generic private sector in our economy. Even with all the justifiable general complaints about the bureaucratic slowness (and not inconsiderable corruption), Polish rules for the registration of private companies, for example, are incomparably more liberal, when contrasted with, for instance, the requirement to obtain licenses from district or county government offices, as is the case in the generally liberal Czech Republic (Benacek 1993).

When we track down the mechanisms of liberalization and deregulation somewhat further, we note the particular significance of the extension of the liberal rule of establishment to both wholesale trade and foreign trade (see Gomułka 1992). Private wholesalers are much quicker than the state-owned mammoths at identifying the products for which there is a large and unsatisfied demand and signal consumers' preferences to the producers. This faster identification of changes in the structure of demand by private wholesalers creates positive stimuli for producers to make changes in the structure of supply. At the same time, the liberalization of foreign trade makes it possible for private wholesalers to import higher quality goods. In addition to the positive stimuli (signaling consumers' preferences) wholesalers therefore convey potential threats. One of these is the possibility of bankruptcy in the event of not adapting to the new higher requirements.

These twofold adaptive pressures affect not only private producers, but also those among SOEs that saw the need to adapt. In this manner, the linkage of private wholesaling with the liberalization of foreign trade becomes a powerful factor contributing to the growth of adaptability and innovativeness in the whole economy. Thus, both aspects of the capitalist market process, errors' elimination and winners' selection (see Pelikan 1985), are simultaneously at work, thanks to the far-reaching freedom of entrepreneurship. This impact has been particularly important for industry, where the high capital threshold makes the process of replacing state-owned enterprises by private ones slower than in other sectors of the economy. (In those sectors where that threshold is not so high, more and more often the only players left in the game are private companies as in construction, commerce, services for enterprises and households.)

If we now wanted to restate the reasons for Poland's success in changing the ownership structure of its economy, we would stress that the successes are owed to those particular features of the transition strategy which have been most strongly criticized by the believers in procrastination as the best strategy of systemic change. Most of them, let it be noted, belong to the 'reformers of the unreformable' (or 'improvers of the unimprovable') from the Polish communist past. Contrary to all the complaints about 'ruining everything' (meaning the state enterprises) and 'excessive openness to imports', it is precisely these features that forced adjustment upon often unwilling producers. To put it in yet another way, the most successful were those developments where economic processes were left to the spontaneous market forces.

Incidentally, herein lies the explanation of the earlier and faster recovery from the 'transformational depression' at the start of transition. Property rights are more secure in the generic private firms. Proper work habits are instilled from the very start. Industrial relations in general are healthy. All this contrasts sharply with the behavioral patterns carried over from the communist past in privatized SOEs. Therefore, efficiency of resource use and production factors employed is generally higher in the former. So is the financial soundness of generic private firms. In consequence, the higher the share of the generic private firms in the aggregate output of the private sector and the smaller the share of the privatized firms, the stronger, more dynamic the recovery. The question is, however, whether the foregoing thesis applies to the whole process of transition from a Soviet-type centrally administered to a capitalist market economy.

It has been a fortuitous coincidence that in Poland strong resistance to privatization 'from above' has been coupled with more decisive removal of the fetters constraining the generic private sector. But in the opinion of these authors the institutional barriers we stress in the report will increasingly circumscribe the growth and diversification opportunities of the private sector. The still-buoyant private sector will increasingly be adversely affected by twofold institutional and policy developments. The spate of regulations intent on controlling a variety of aspects of business activities through licensing, quality and other controls, concessions, ill-regulated environmental standards, etc. – all these increase output costs directly and indirectly – directly through compliance costs and indirectly through corruption costs. These are topped by ever-more costly labor regulations that strongly discourage compliance and result in shifting a part of business activities from the registered to the unregistered (gray) economy; by the capriciousness of the tax regulations and decisions; as well as by the disadvantaged position of the private sector *vis-à-vis* other public authorities (with respect to public procurement, etc.).

While regulation throttles the private sector's vitality and increases its cost, the continuous existence of the substantial – and in some sectors still dominant – public sector limits the opportunities for expansion of the private sector in a more roundabout manner. There are several layers of this roundabout effect on the prospects of the private sector. The first layer is the political imbalance between the economically dominant and more efficient private sector and economically less-efficient, largely unreconstructed public sector. The very size of the latter and its inability and/or sheer unwillingness to adjust to the requirements of the market economy creates demand for financial resources to support the loss-makers. These resources are more often than not granted to the loss-makers as the public sector is politically over-represented. The two dominant political camps, the ex-communists and 'Solidarity', as stressed earlier, draw their strength from the same segments of the economy: large state enterprises and budget-financed public services (health, education, etc.). Given the fact that the economically more efficient private sector is politically under-represented, economic rationale for more efficiency-based allocation criteria often gives ground to the political expediency of support for their own political supporters.

This political expediency results in a variety of more or less overt forms of support:

1 Direct budget subsidies. These, given their high visibility, are rather small and not used very often;
2 Indirect grant- or loan-type support from a variety of state agencies. As these are more difficult to track by the opposition and even more by the interested public, they play an increasing role in maintaining the inefficiency of the public sector;
3 Indirect budget subsidies in the form of government guarantees. The budgetary allocations for the purpose have been rapidly increasing of late and their allocation among recipients shows a strong bias in favor of large heavy-industry SOEs having political clout;

4 Indirect tax concessions through tolerated non-payment of taxes and social security contributions by many large SOEs or outright forgiveness of the unpaid taxes, contributions and accrued interest.
5 Pressure on state-owned banks to support politically important state-owned loss-makers directly, through new loans, or indirectly, through partial forgiveness of past loans within the framework of the debt restructuring loans.

All these measures of support substantially soften the budget constraint of state mammoths and make them even less willing to undergo the necessary adjustment (including closures of some SOEs that do not give any hope of leaving the list of persistent loss-makers). However, their adverse impact is much wider than on mammoths themselves. They create an economic equivalent of the cosmic black hole, gluttonizing the financial resources necessary elsewhere in the economy. First, these are needed by the expanding private sector for which the continuous existence of the black hole reduces even further the opportunity to benefit from the services of the banking sector ('even further' because small and medium-sized firms are generally disadvantaged *vis-à-vis* large ones in their relations with banks and most financial institutions). Second, these resources could be used for the inevitable institutional changes in the social security system, especially the pension system (see the previous chapter).

Over time, the still rapidly expanding private sector may at best slow down considerably and at worst decline under the twofold impact of the increasingly costly burden of regulation and continuing existence of the unprivatized, highly-subsidized state enterprise sector. The question is how such adverse trends are to be avoided. To answer it, we are forced to move from the economics of transition to the political economy of transition.

A look at the post-1989 history is not at all encouraging, especially with respect to the necessary drastic reduction of the state enterprise sector through privatization and the imposition of the market rules of the game on the remaining unprivatized public enterprises. Given the political over-representation of SOEs, neither non-communist governments formed by the Solidarity camp, nor subsequent post-communist governments have exerted strong pressure on state enterprises to adjust. In fact, the post-communists, devoid of any serious ideological preferences and intent only on remaining in power and using the state for personal gain, made political favoritism the cornerstone of their politics of postponing or avoiding institutional change. For it is political favoritism that gains votes and it is the *conditio sine qua non* of being able to live off the state.

Such a policy, if it is going to be successful, assumes that further institution-building in the transition process is unwelcome by a sufficiently large body of the electorate. Public opinion surveys in the last few years largely support such an assumption. As quoted already in Chapter 1, a 1995 public opinion survey showed that liberal capitalist order is criticized by 70 percent of the electorate of the post-communist SLD, by 73 percent of the backward-looking peasant party electorate (PSL) and by almost 80 percent of the Solidarity electorate! Thus, it is criticized from both ends of the political spectrum. The foregoing leads us to the conclusion that the spectrum of economic philosophies is U-shaped, like the Hannah Arendt spectrum of political philosophies. Therefore, the distance between left wing views on the economy and their lack of acceptance of capitalism, and right wing views and their lack of acceptance of capitalism is much smaller than the distance between both and the center that actively promotes or at least acquiesces to capitalism. This, however, may be the general rule. A typically post-communist country problem is that both wings are usually relatively strong *vis-à-vis* the center (which, in Western societies, gets some 70–90 percent of the vote).

It is worthwhile identifying the main determinants of such criticism of, and resistance to, the capitalist market order to evaluate the probability of a shift of opinion that will allow a resumption of systemic change in the future. The source of the strong support of the parties and groupings that criticize post-1989 systemic change lies first of all, in the opinion of the present writers, in the erosion of moral order brought about by half a century of communism. Large state enterprises were the monuments of waste. The distance between what was trumpeted as achievements by propaganda and reported to higher levels of hierarchy and what was there in reality was greater than elsewhere in communist economies. At the same time better rewards than elsewhere for more fiction than elsewhere added to cynicism and demoralization. Xymena Gliszczyńska (1994), a labor psychologist, wrote about the shift of the locus of *lumpenproletariat* from the margin of the society to large state enterprises. By the same token, we may use the term *lumpenintelligentsia* with respect to a substantial group of professionals and white collar workers in general, educated under communism. Thus, in Western societies and in East European ones before the advent of communism, those who acquired formal education and began a professional career entered at the same time a given professional group that maintained its own professional standards and moral codes. The assault of communism very quickly liquidated autonomous professional associations and later eroded the codes themselves.

The greater the passage of time away from the normal world, its standards and codes, the greater was the demoralization of *lumpenintelligentsia* that never knew any other world than that of communism. The case of workers from large state enterprises (the new *lumpenproletariat*) was the same. In a rather large number of cases, people learned to do without standards and codes, especially as they turned out to be an obstacle rather than help in obtaining higher pay and promotion. The systemic change brought these habits to an end or at the very least, threatened to do so in the not-too-distant future. Demoralized professionals and white collar workers faced not only demands from their new superiors for better work but also a prospect that their juniors, who have not had enough time to become demoralized by the Soviet system, will soon replace them in their rather badly paid but also undemanding jobs. And in the medium term there has been the prospect of thousands of talented and diligent youngsters finishing better schools than those they attended themselves (often paying in private schools for their education) and working with skill and enthusiasm in the environment that rewarded talent, skills, risk-taking, and hard work.

Those demoralized by the old regime soon after the start of transition began looking for a political representation that would promise them a return to the past or at least the substantial slow-down of the transition process. We are reminded by Douglass North (1979), a recent Nobel laureate in economics, that there are winners and losers in economic activity and that those who lose in the market often do not adjust but turn to politics to regain what they have lost.

It is not necessary that they *actually* lose. It is enough that they feel the threat of a loss or even have a feeling of uncertainty. Thus, people may talk of crisis even in the face of increasing living standards, as was the case of a majority of households in Poland in transition, not because they were worse off but because we live through times when 'the future appears most uncertain and can hardly be ascertained by extrapolating past trends' (Giersch 1995). This feeling of uncertainty has been reinforced by the perceptions of capitalism people held at the start of transition. As stressed by Szymanderski (1996) in the previously-quoted paper, those perceptions have been formed by the ever-dimmer intergenerational transmission of the images of the past normality and by largely superficial encounters with the West. The promise of the return to the mainstream or to 'normal economic standards of the West' was largely understood as the promise of a dramatic improvement in living standards, given what people saw in Western shops (without working in Western factories and offices).

The fact that such an improvement has been predicated upon structural changes preceding it, associated redundancies and even enterprise closures; on productivity increases; reduction of resource costs; elimination of sloppiness, shirking, and theft; as well as many other determinants of success, has hardly been taken into account. The fact that there have been identifiable losers or that the improvement in living standards (although significant) was not dramatic, added to frustration, disorientation, and reinforced the search for alternatives – even phony or fraudulent ones. It is not surprising, for example, that almost 90 percent of those who, in the 1990 presidential elections, voted for an economic charlatan (Tyminski), voted in 1995 for Kwaśniewski.

The completion of the transition to a capitalist market economy is, however, necessary if Poland is not to end up in the middle of nowhere. An over-regulated, over-centralized, and arbitrarily-managed economy will not perform even with tolerable levels of efficiency (to say nothing about catching up with the community of countries we aspire to join). The institutional barriers analyzed in the report, if not removed, are going to exert an ever greater adverse influence on Polish economic performance.

To quote North (1979) again, in predatory economic systems there are two determinants of institutional (property rights) structure: interests of the ruling stratum and the cost reduction of maintaining the economic system, necessary for its survival. The inefficient institutions may survive for quite some time if they are benefiting the ruling stratum. But over time the pressure for their change is going to build up as efficiency deteriorates and well-being declines. Let us add: especially if the free elections are maintained. Changes in the voting pattern may then result.

Thus, the logic of the foregoing analysis suggests that things will get worse before they get better. Once they get worse, the well known dictum of American businessman and politician George Schultz, applies: 'If things get bad enough, people will do even the most obvious and sensible things'. Hence, there is room for medium-term optimism.

LITERATURE

SPECIAL REPORTS

Papers specially prepared for or published in connection with this report and all issued by the Adam Smith Research Center, Warsaw.

Chmiel, J. and Pawłowska, Z. (1996) 'Zmiany w strukturze własności: sektor prywatny w gospodarce polskiej w latach 1990–1994' [Changes in the structure of ownership: the private sector in the Polish economy, 1990–1994], Working Paper No. 19.

Frieske, K.W. and Machol-Zajda, L. (1995) 'Dynamika konfliktu przemysłowego: spory zbiorowe i strajki w Polsce, 1989–1994' [The dynamics of industrial conflict in Poland, 1989–1994], typescript.

Gilowska, Z. (1995) 'Decentralizacja terytorialna a aktywizacja gospodarki' [Territorial self-government and economic dynamism], Working Paper No. 2.

Góra, M., Socha, W.M. and Sztanderska, U. (1995) 'Zachowania bezrobotnych na rynku pracy' [Behavior of the unemployed on the labor market], Working Paper No. 5.

Hockuba, Z. and Płachecki, A. (1996) 'Rozwój rynku kapitałowego a proces prywatyzacji w Polsce' [The development of capital markets and privatization], Working Paper No. 13.

Kamiński, A.Z. and Stefanowicz, J. (1996) 'Jak buduje się Trzecią Rzeczpospolitą: Ułomne reguły gry' [How the Third Republic is built: distorted rules of the game], Working Paper No. 9.

Markowska, H. and Kubalczak, P. (1995) 'Europejska Karta Społeczna a ubezpieczenia społeczne w Polsce' [The European Social Charter and the social security system in Poland], typescript.

Mech, C. (1995) 'Konieczność powstania funduszy emerytalnych' [The necessity of pension funds], Working Paper No. 8.

—— (1996) 'Finanse ubezpieczeń emerytalno-rentowych w Polsce' [Financing the pension system and its change], typescript.

Mickiewicz, T. (1995) 'Nierównowaga praw i obowiązków pracy i kapitału:

Polska w okresie transformacji systemowej' [Imbalance between labor and capital during Polish transformation], Working Paper No. 3.

—— (1996) 'Rozwiązania instytucjonalne służące redukcji naturalnej stopy bezrobocia' [Institutional measures reducing the natural rate of unemployment], Working Paper No. 20.

Pinera, J. (1995) 'Bagno ubezpieczeń społecznych' [The social security mess], Working Paper No. 4.

—— (1996) 'Teraz ubezpieczenia społeczne!' [Social security reform – now], booklet.

Pretkiel, W. and Zalewska, H. (1995) 'Zmiany na rynku pracy a świadczenia społeczne' [Changes in the labor market and payments from Social Security], typescript.

Rutkowski, J. (1995) 'Przetasowanie płac: Zmiany struktury wynagrodzeń w okresie transformacji gospodarczej' [Relative wage changes during the transformation process], Working Paper No. 7.

Szymanderski, J. (1996) 'Stosunek opinii publicznej do zmian instytucjonalnych w Polsce' [Public opinion on institutional change], Working Paper No. 23.

Szymkiewicz, K. (1996) 'Wnioski z doświadczeń innych krajów dla rozwoju gospodarczego Polski' [Other countries' experience: some conclusions for Poland's economic development], Working Paper No. 26.

'Uczestnictwo w rynku światowym a wzrost gospodarczy' [Participation in the world market] (1996), Working Paper No. 11.

Wellisz, S. (1996) 'Czy Polsce potrzebna jest polityka przemysłowa?' [Does Poland need industrial policy?], Working Paper No. 16.

Wilczyński, W. (1996) 'Ustrój gospodarczy i system regulacji w Polsce: Wpływ na stabilizację i wzrost gospodarczy' [The economic system and regulation in Poland], Working Paper No. 18.

Winiecki, J. (1995) 'Jak zrobić program masowej prywatyzacji nie realizując niemal żadnych istotnych jej celów (doświadczenia polskiego PPP)' [How to make a mass privatization program without accomplishing any important aims (the experience of Polish MPP)], Working Paper No. 6.

Zamrazilova, E. (1996) 'Rynek pracy w Republice Czeskiej w procesie transformacji' [The labor market in the Czech Republic], Working Paper No. 15.

'Zmiany w regulacjach stosunków gospodarczych w latach 1989–1994' [Changes in economic regulation in 1989–1994] (1995), survey by the law firm 'Juris', typescript.

REFERENCES

Balcerowicz, L. (1993) 'Common fallacies in the debate on economic transition in Central and Eastern Europe', EBRD Working Paper No. 10, London.

Beksiak, J. (1993) 'Zmiany systemowe a teoria ekonomii' 28 października [Intervention at the conference on systemic change and economic theory, 28 October], Warsaw.

Beksiak, J., Grzelońska, U., Rybczynski, T., and Winiecki, J. (1991) 'List otwarty do Prezydenta Rzeczypospolitej w sprawie gespodarki' [open letter on the economy to the President of the Republic of Poland], *Rzeczpospolita*, October 10.

Benacek, V. (1993) 'The toil and trouble of an indigenous entrepreneur during transition: the case of the Czech Republic', Center for Economic Research and Graduate Education, Charles University, Prague, September, mimeo.

Bobińska, K. (1994) 'Sytuacja sektora przedsiębiorstw' [Situation of the enterprise sector], Koniunktura gospodarcza Polski, Bulletin No. 1, Adam Smith Research Center, Warsaw.

Bruno, M. (1992) 'Stabilization and reform in Eastern Europe: a preliminary evaluation', *IMF Staff Papers*, vol. 39, no. 4.

Burda, M. (1993) 'Unemployment, labour markets and structural change in Eastern Europe', *Economic Policy*, no. 16, April.

Csaba, L. (1994) 'The political economy of free trade regimes in Central Europe', Centre for Economic Policy Research discussion paper 1017, London.

Dziadul, J. (1995) 'Jaja na węglu: Emocje wokół górniczych zarobków powracają niczym bumerang' [Emotions surrounding miners' earnings come back], *Polityka*, no. 13.

Eliasson, G. (1987) 'Technological competition and trade in the experimentally organized economy', Industrial Institute for Economic and Social Research, Stockholm.

Flanagan, R.J. (1991) 'Wages and Wage Policies in Market Economies', Joint OECD & ILO Working Paper, International Labour Organization, Geneva.

Giersch, H. (1995) 'Economic Dynamism: Lessons from German Experience', Prepared for the First International Hayek Memorial Conference, Vienna, 15–17 March, mimeo.

Gliszczyńska, X. (1994) 'Psychologiczne bariery pozytywnych efektów prywatyzacji', [Psychological barriers to the positive effects of privatization], in 'Monitoring procesów prywatyzacyjnych 1992–94' [Monitoring of Privatization Processes 1992–94], Adam Smith Research Center, Warsaw, mimeo.

Gomułka, S. (1992) 'On the design of economic policy' in 'Debate on the Transition of Post-communist Economies', *Acta Oeconomica*, vol. 44, nos 3–4.

—— (1995): 'Połowiczna reforma czy antyreforma?' [Half a reform or antireform?], *Życie Gospodarcze*, No. 24.

Góra, M. (1994) 'Rynek pracy w Polsce. Pierwsze lata transformacji – próba analizy' [The labor market in Poland. The first years of transformation], Studies and analyses of the Center for Economic and Social Reserch (CASE), Warsaw.

Gruszecki, T. and Winiecki, J. (1991) 'Privatization in East-Central Europe: a comparative perspective', *Aussenwirtschaft*, vol. 46, no. 1.

Hayek, F.A. (1973) *Law, Legislation and Liberty, Volume I: Rules and Order*, University of Chicago Press, Chicago.

Hirschman, A.O. (1963) *Journeys Toward Progress: Studies of Economic Policy-Making in Latin America*, Twentieth Century Fund, New York.

LITERATURE

Hockuba, Z. (1995) 'Droga do spontanicznego porządku. Transformacja systemowa w świetle problemu regulacji' [A road toward spontaneous order], PWN, Warsaw.

Kamiński, A.Z. and Kurczewska, J. (1994) 'Institutional Transformations in Poland: The Rise of Nomadic Political Elites', in Alestalo, M. et al. (eds) *The Transformation of Europe: Social Conditions and Consequences*, IFIS Publications, Warsaw.

Kornai, J. (1979) 'Resource-constrained versus demand-constrained systems', *Econometrica*, vol. 47, no. 4.

—— (1986) 'The soft budget constraint', *Kyklos*, vol. 33, no. 1.

—— (1992) 'The postsocialist transition and the State: reflections in the light of Hungarian fiscal problems', *American Economic Review*, vol. 82, no. 2.

—— (1993) 'Transformational recession: a general phenomenon examined through the example of Hungary's development', Collegium Budapest discussion papers, No. 1, June.

Koronowski, A. (1994) 'Miękki budżet' [The 'soft' budget], *Życie Gospodarcze*, No. 51.

Kostrzewa, W. (1994) [Untitled article on privatization of the banking sector in Poland – the current status and prospects], *Zeszyty PBR–CASE*, No. 13, Warsaw.

Levy, B. (1993) 'An institutional analysis of the design and sequence of trade and investment policy reform', *World Bank Economic Review*, vol. 7, no. 2.

McKenzie, R. (1985) *Competing Visions: The Political Conflict over America's Future*, CATO Institute, Washington DC.

North, D.C. (1979) 'A framework for analyzing the State in economic history', *Explorations in Economic History*, vol. 16, July.

OECD (1995) 'Poland', Annual Report, Paris.

Olson, M. (1965) *The Logic of Collective Action. Public Goods and a Theory of Groups*, Harvard University Press, Cambridge, MA.

—— (1980) *The Rise and Decline of Nations. Economic Growth, Stagflation and Social Rigidities*, Yale University Press, New Haven, CT.

Painter, F.M. and Rourke, R.J. (1993) 'Policy and intitutional considerations in equity market development', in Walters, A. and Hanke, S. (eds) *Capital Markets and Development*, Institute for Contemporary Studies Press, San Francisco.

Pejovich, S. (1990) *The Economics of Property Rights: Towards a Theory of Comparative Systems*, Kluwer, Dordrecht.

Pelikan, P. (1985) 'Private enterprise vs. government control: an organizationally dynamic comparison', Industrial Institute of Economic and Social Research, Stockholm, January, mimeo.

Phelps, E.S. (1994) 'Non-wage employment subsidies versus the welfare state', *American Economic Review*, vol. 84, no. 2, May.

Płoch, J. (1995) 'Pożytki z upadłości' [Benefits of bankruptcy], *Kapitalista Powszechny*, No. 2 (37).

PPRG Report (1993) 'Economic Policy of Poland', PPRG Group, University of Warsaw, July.

Pretkiel, W. (1994) 'Skala przyszłych zobowiązań' [The pension system: scale of future financial commitments], *Życie Gospodarcze*, No. 50.

107

LITERATURE

Prowse, M. (1993) 'The Asian Miracle that was not', *Financial Times*, September 27.

Stefanowicz, J. (1996) 'Uwagi do projektu ustawy o łączeniu i grupowaniu niektórych banków działających w formie spółki akcyjnej (druk nr 1468)'. 'Expert opinion prepared for the parliamentary representation of the Freedom Union Party (Unia Wolności)', mimeo.

Stefanowicz, J. and Winiecki, J. (1994) 'Zamówienia dla wybranych' [Procurement contracts for the privileged], *Wprost*, No. 40.

Surażska, W. (1996) 'Wybory prezydenckie 1990 i 1995. Analiza porównawcza w przekroju terytorialnym' [Presidential elections in 1990 and 1995: spatial analysis], Material presented at the Adam Smith Research Centre conference, Warsaw, mimeo.

Topiński, W., (interview with) (1996) 'Szara przyszłość. Każda reforma systemu emerytalnego musi być rozciągnięta na kilkadziesiąt lat', [The gray future: every pension system reform must be stretched for dozens of years] *Cash*, No. 10.

Trybunal Konstytucyjny [The Constitutional Tribunal] (1991) 'Orzeczenie pełnego składu Trybunału Konstytucyjnego z dnia 11 lutego 1992r. wraz z uzasadnieniem w sprawie połączonych wniosków dotyczących Ustawy Emerytalnej' [Ruling of the Contitutional Tribunal concerning the Pension Bill], Sygnatura Akt K. 14/1991, Warsaw.

Walters, A. and Hanke, S. (eds) (1993) *Capital Markets and Development*, ICS Press, Institute for Contemporary Studies, San Francisco.

Wiktorow, A. (1994) 'Prawa nabyte i oczekiwane' [Acquired rights and expectations], *Życie Gospodarcze*, No. 50.

Wilczyński, W. (1994) 'Samorząd terytorialny: Zachcianka czy konieczność' [Territorial self-government: whim or necessity], *Życie Gospodarcze*, No. 51.

Winiecki, J. (1988) 'Narrow wage differentials between blue-collar and white-collar workers and excess demand for manual labour in the CPEs: causally linked system-specific phenomena', *Osteuropa Wirtschaft*, No. 3.

―― (1989) 'How to get the ball rolling', *Financial Times*, 13 January.

―― (1990a) 'No capitalism minus capitalists', *Financial Times*, 20 June.

―― (1990b) 'Post-Soviet-type economies in transition: what have we learned from the Polish transition programme in its rirst year', *Weltwirtschaftliches Archiv*, vol. 126, no. 4.

―― (1991) 'The inevitability of a fall of output in the early stages of transition to the market: theoretical underpinning', *Soviet Studies*, vol. 43, no. 4.

―― (1993a) 'Polityka-gospodarka-perspektywy biznesu' [Politics, economics and business prospects], *Kapitalista Powszechny*, no. 9 (28), July 5.

―― (1993b) 'Knowledge of Soviet-type economy and "Heterodox" stabilization-based outcomes in Eastern Europe', *Weltwirtschaftliches Archiv*, vol. 129, no. 2.

―― (1995a): 'The applicability of standard reform packages to Eastern Europe', *Journal of Comparative Economics*, vol. 20, no. 2.

―― (1995b) 'Foreign investments in Eastern Europe: expectations, trends, policies', Paper presented at the conference 'Integration der Europaischen Union und Herausforderungen der koreanischen Wirtschaft' in Seoul, 29 September.

—— (1996) 'Ruch lawinowy: Koalicja dzieli i rządzi' [Corruption avalanche: the ruling coalition divides and rules], *Polityka*, No. 7.

Winiecki, E.D. and Winiecki, J. (1992) *The Structural Legacy of the Soviet-Type Economy. A Collection of Papers*, Centre for Research into Communist Economies, London.

Witkowski, J. (1995) *Labour Market in Poland in 1994: New trends, old problems*, Central Statistical Office, Warsaw.

World Bank (1994) *Averting the Old-Age Crisis: Policies to protect the old and promote growth*, World Bank Research Publications/Oxford University Press, New York.

Zamrazilova, E. (1994) 'Labour Market', [A snowball effect: the ruling coalition divides and rules] Institute of Economic Studies, Charles University, Prague, Reform Round Table Working Paper No. 15, mimeo.

Zieliński, M. (1994) 'Dobrowolny przymus: Reforma systemu bankowego ma na celu zmusić banki do finansowania inwestycji, które wskaże rząd', [A 'Voluntary Coercion': On Governmental Aims of Reform of the Banking System], *Wprost*, no. 44.

INDEX